The Heritage Book

1985

Edna McCann

Collier Macmillan Canada, Inc.

Collier Macmillan Canada, Inc.
50 Gervais Drive
Don Mills, Ontario

ISBN 02.947110.9

Printed and bound in Hong Kong by
Scanner Art Services Inc. Toronto

Ninth Edition

Introduction

It is hard to believe that this year marks the halfway point in the decade. It seems as though it was only last year that the 1980s began. How much has happened in the last few years, how many exciting developments have taken place, how much we have to look forward to!

Yet in spite of the breathtaking speed of change these days, I find from my reading, my letters, and my conversations with friends and strangers, that people change really very little. Family and friends are still most important. Values like courage, kindness, tolerance, hard work, and honesty are still highly esteemed. Young people still dream dreams, and all of us maintain faith and hope in the future, just as we did when I was young.

Perhaps the challenge facing us in the second half of the 1980s is to learn how we can preserve and honour those things we feel to be truly important at the same time as our skills and imaginations change the world we live in.

May *The Heritage Book 1985* provide you with many happy moments, and may the coming year be one of joy for you.

Edna McCann

PICTURE CREDITS

Winter
- Keith Greatrix
- Patrick Gallagher
- Patrick Gallagher
- Patrick Gallagher
- Keith Greatrix
- Patrick Gallagher

Spring
- Keith Greatrix
- Keith Greatrix
- Patrick Gallagher
- Patrick Gallagher
- Patrick Gallagher
- Patrick Gallagher

Summer
- Patrick Gallagher
- Patrick Gallagher
- Patrick Gallagher
- Keith Greatrix
- Keith Greatrix
- Patrick Gallagher

Autumn
- Patrick Gallagher
- Patrick Gallagher
- Keith Greatrix
- Patrick Gallagher
- Keith Greatrix
- Patrick Gallagher

Cover photo: Birgitte Nielson

January

Tuesday — January 1

I rejoice in my life because the lamp still glows;
I seek no thorny ways;
I love the small pleasures of life.
If the doors are too low I bend;
If I can remove a stone from the path, I do so;
If it is too heavy, I go round it.
I find something every day that pleases me.
The cornerstone, my belief in God, makes my heart glad and my face shining.

I feel that this poem by the mother of Goethe, the great German thinker, is a very appropriate way to begin a new year. Let us rejoice in our lives, find something to please us in each day, and greet the New Year with glad hearts and shining faces.

Wednesday — January 2

Now that the festive season has slipped by once again, I enjoy sitting quietly by the fire and passing through the hectic days again — this time at a slower pace. So often my visits with my grandchildren and great-grandchildren seem to be a blur at the time. It is only later that I can really sit back and think about our conversations in depth.

It is very enjoyable to talk to young people. When you are as old as I am you wonder if ideas and values have changed over these many years. I am usually very astonished at how little change there has been. What I do find is that young people seem to acquire their ideals and their values at a much earlier age. Children are encouraged to express their own opinions and to question others' ideas and opinions. No longer are children seen and not heard. They are listened to and respected as thinking people who have ideas to contribute.

This evening I plan to sit by the fire with a cup of tea and think about my time spent with Mickey, my great-grandchild — and our aspiring astronaut. I enjoyed it last week, I'm sure I will enjoy it again this evening.

Thursday — January 3

Man is the only animal that laughs and weeps; for he is the only animal that is struck with the difference between what things are and what they might have been.

— *William Hazlitt*

Friday — January 4

The heart's affections are divided like the branches of the cedar tree; if the tree loses one strong branch, it will suffer but it does not die. It will pour all its vitality into the next branch so that it will grow and fill the empty place.

— *Kahlil Gibran*

Saturday — January 5

Doing the best you can with the little opportunities that come along will get you farther than idly wishing for the big chance that may never arrive.

Sunday — January 6

This Sunday is the Epiphany, or the commemoration of the coming of the Three Wise Men.

As with gladness men of old
Did the guiding star behold,
As with joy they hailed its light,
Leading onward, beaming bright,
So most gracious Lord may we
Ever more be led by Thee.
As they offered gifts most rare
At the cradle rude and bare,
So may we with holy joy,
Pure and free from sin's alloy,
All our costliest treasures bring,
Christ, to Thee our Heavenly King.

Monday — January 7

An elderly gentleman in our nearby nursing home recently celebrated his 100th birthday.

Passing this milestone is a very newsworthy event and a local television reporter was interviewing Mr. Howard on this momentous occasion.

"Are you able to get out and walk much?" he was asked.

"Why I can certainly walk better today than I could a hundred years ago," he answered with a grin.

TUESDAY — JANUARY 8

JAKE Frampton stopped by today and he brought with him a Christmas gift from one of his nephews. He was so proud as he showed me what this young fellow had made for him.

It was a hand-carved and polished walking stick. I don't think that I have ever seen a more beautiful stick anywhere.

"You know, Edna, young Jack has always been very thoughtful and sensitive. Even as a boy he showed a great sensitivity to the needs of others. He was often doing things for his elderly next-door neighbour — little things, like shovelling her walk without being asked, or putting on her storm windows in the fall.

"This past summer, after the fall I took down the steps at the cottage, I needed to use a cane for a while. Jack must have known how much I disliked having to use it and in his usual thoughtful way he has made using a walking aid a joy instead of a nuisance. I am so lucky to have this boy as a nephew!"

Wednesday — January 9

Emily sent me a most delightful letter from her winter home in Florida. Emily's letters are always a ray of sunshine on any day, but on dull cold January days they are particularly welcome.

Emily is a person who never seems to have an idle minute. In her letter today she tells me about a new project of hers in the south. Emily and a few of her condominium neighbours have started a number of classes to interest grandchildren who are visiting in their complex. Because it is an adult area and the children who visit are often uncomfortable with the numerous rules and regulations, Emily and her friends take turns doing things that the children enjoy.

For example, Tom McArthur takes the children fishing on the pier each morning before the swimming pool opens. Peg Smith and Mary Reynolds are teaching cooking and baking some afternoons, and Emily runs an arts and crafts program.

The grandparents and the children seem to be enjoying their visits much more and adults and children alike seem to enjoy getting to know one another better.

Thursday — January 10

George Bernard Shaw had a sense of humour that appeals greatly to me. I enjoyed this story that Jake told me recently.

Mr. Shaw was having lunch in a restaurant in London one day. The orchestra played one noisy song after another without intermission.

Finally summoning the head waiter, Mr. Shaw enquired, "Does the band do requests?"

"Certainly sir," replied the headwaiter.

"Excellent! Would you please ask them to play dominoes until I have finished eating."

Friday — January 11

If a task is once begun,
Never leave it till it's done.
Be the labour great or small
Do it well or not at all.

Saturday — January 12

A mistake is at least evidence that someone tried to do something.

SUNDAY — JANUARY 13

CHRIST, our Saviour, come Thou to dwell within us,
That we may go forth with the light of thy hope in our eyes and thy faith and love in our hearts.

MONDAY — JANUARY 14

God's Pledge to You

NOT cloudless days;
Not rose-strewn ways;
Not care-free years,
Devoid of sorrow's tears —
But strength to bear
Your load of human care,
And grace to live aright
And keep your raiment white,
And love to see you through;
That is God's pledge to you.

TUESDAY — JANUARY 15

MAN must evolve for all human conflict a method which rejects revenge, aggression, and retaliation. The foundation of such a method is love.

— *Martin Luther King, Jr.*

Wednesday — January 16

My grandson Fred and his wife June stopped by this evening. They live out in the country so I was quite surprised by their unexpected visit.

They had been to see June's grandmother, who is in hospital recovering from a broken hip.

Her injury brought to mind the many dangers that this time of year brings to us older folks.

Although ice and snowy conditions pose a hazard to everyone, they are particularly dangerous to seniors because most of us are not as sure of our footing as we once were.

Probably the most serious problem is snow on the sidewalks where no shovelling has been done. Although most people are very conscientious about snow removal, all you need is one area where it has not been shovelled and I, for one, find it very difficult to walk. If everyone realized how many of us no longer drive and are obliged to walk while carrying parcels, I'm sure that they would make an effort to clear their walks.

Marg, Bruce, and I are fortunate to have our young neighbour lads to shovel for us. They do a splendid job each snowfall.

Thursday — January 17

I know an older lady who seemed to have more than her share of trouble and hard times. Nevertheless she is always cheerful and happy. When she was asked the secret of her cheerfulness she replied, "Well, you see it's like this. The Bible says, 'And it came to pass.' It never says 'And it came to stay'."

Friday — January 18

My husband George and I were married at a very young age, so when my friend Janice Ragwell came to me a few years ago, worried about her young son's impending marriage I was able to reassure her that in some cases young marriages do work.

Janice came over to visit yesterday and to tell me of another young couple's wedding that she attended. When the minister asked the bridegroom to repeat, "With all my worldly goods I thee endow," the groom's father chuckled audibly, "Well, there goes his motor bike."

SATURDAY — JANUARY 19

ELINOR Wylie wrote this beautiful poem about the winter snows.

Let us walk in the white snow
  In a soundless space;
With footsteps quiet and slow,
  At a tranquil pace,
    Under veils of white lace.
I shall go shod in silk,
  and you in wool,
White as a white cow's milk,
  More beautiful
Than the breast of a gull.

We shall walk through the still town
  In a windless peace;
We shall step upon white down,
  Upon silver fleece
Upon softer than these.

We shall walk in velvet shoes:
  Wherever we go
Silence will fall like dews
  On white silence below.
We shall walk in the snow.

Sunday — January 20

BELOVED, follow not that which is evil, but that which is good. He that doeth good is of God: but he that doeth evil hath not seen God.

— *III John 11*

Monday — January 21

WHEN you have grown up in a minister's family you learn the meaning of the word "thrift" at a very early age.

My mother had some oft-used expressions that we heard regularly. Here are a few of her favourites.

Keep adding little to little, and soon there will be a great heap.

— *Virgil*

Wilful waste brings wilful want.

— *Thomas Fuller*

Bad spending makes the poor poorer.

— *Hartley Withers*

Teach economy, that is one of the first virtues.

— *Abraham Lincoln*

Tuesday — January 22

My daughter Marg is a splendid cook! She loves to cook and bake and she is extremely innovative. Marg enjoys taking old recipes and making changes to create delightful new dishes.

Bruce, her husband, is a joy to cook for. He attacks each new dish with gusto and it's a rare time that he doesn't finish off his entire dinner and come back for seconds.

Unfortunately, his pleasure has been diminished lately by the noticeable expansion of his middle.

Last week when he loosened his belt for the second time he decided that the day of reckoning had arrived.

Since then Marg has been cooking small measured portions of fish and chicken to be served along with steamed vegetables and salads.

Bruce has been very vocal in his complaints. He wanders around mumbling about "rabbit food" and "starving" and "feeling faint."

In actual fact he has already lost almost five pounds and he looks and feels much better.

Next week things will probably be back to normal and the word "delicious" will once again be heard in this home.

Wednesday — January 23

I have always thought that the telephone is one of the greatest blessings of modern life. It brings close to hand a whole company of friends and relatives, along with countless services.

But for some weeks now in the evening hours I have been called by some sweet young voice, or, worse yet, a computer voice, trying to sell everything from rug cleaners to toiletries.

Last night was the worst! A cemetery company called to try to sell me a plot of land for my burial.

I found it very difficult not to be rude to the young woman, but I do object to commercial enterprises using my private phone as a means of access to my home.

I am sure that I am not alone in these feelings. I suppose that very little can be done to curb this practice but maybe if few enough of us use the services solicited, the telephone will not be used in this manner.

Thursday — January 24

A lost battle is a battle one thinks one has lost.

— *Marshall Foch*

Friday — January 25

My heart's in the Highlands,
my heart is not here
My heart's in the Highlands a-chasing the deer;
Chasing the wild deer, and following the roe,
My heart's in the Highlands wherever I go.
Farewell to the Highlands, farewell to the North,
The birthplace of valour, the country of worth;
Wherever I wander, wherever I rove,
The hills of the Highlands forever I love.
Farewell to the mountains high covered with snow
Farewell to the straths and green valleys below
Farewell to the forests and wild-hanging woods
Farewell to the torrents and loud–pouring flood.
My heart's in the Highlands, my heart is not here;
My heart's in the Highlands a-chasing the deer
Chasing the wild deer, and following the roe
My heart's in the Highlands wherever I go.

On Robbie Burns Day, this poem is certainly a fitting tribute to his native Scotland.

Saturday — January 26

A smile is a very inexpensive way to improve your looks.

Sunday — January 27

Unto thee, O Lord, do I lift up my soul.
O my God, I trust in thee:
Let me not be ashamed,
Let not mine enemies triumph over me.
Yea, let none that wait on thee be ashamed:
Let them be ashamed which transgress without cause.
Show me thy ways, O Lord;
Teach me thy paths.

— *Psalm 25:1–4*

Monday — January 28

"Your children won't remember if their house was all neat, but they will remember if you read them stories."

How true that is! Although neatness in a home is important, it certainly should not be so time consuming or important that it precludes time spent enjoying the children.

Tuesday — January 29

His thoughts were slow, his words were few, and never formed to glisten, but he was a joy to all his friends — you should have heard him listen!

Wednesday — January 30

To live long, it is necessary to live slowly.

— *Cicero*

Thursday — January 31

Here it is the end of January and we're still cleaning up from Christmas. Last week we cleaned out our chequing account and this week we cleaned out our savings account.

February

Friday — February 1

'Tis winter now, the fallen snow
Has left the heavens all coldly clear.
Through lifeless boughs the sharp winds blow,
And all the earth is dread and drear.

And yet God's love is not withdrawn
His life within the keen air breathes
His beauty paints the crimson dawn
And clothes the boughs with glittering wreaths

— *Henry Wadsworth Longfellow*

Saturday — February 2

I'm sixty five and I guess that puts me with geriatrics, but if there were fifteen months in every year I'd only be forty eight.

— *James Thurber*

Sunday — February 3

Make a joyful noise unto the Lord, all ye lands.
Serve the Lord with gladness: come before his presence with singing.
Know ye that the Lord he is God: it is he that hath made us, and not we ourselves; we are his people, and the sheep of his pasture.
Enter into his gates with thanksgiving, and into his courts with praise: be thankful unto him, and bless his name.
For the Lord is good; his mercy is everlasting; and his truth endureth to all generations.

— *Psalm 100*

Monday — February 4

My granddaughter Phyllis and her husband Bill stopped by this weekend with some very exciting news. They are expecting a baby in July.

I have never seen Phyllis looking more radiant. They are both so excited that it is comical to listen to them. It's as if they are the first people in the world to have a baby, but as I think back George and I behaved exactly the same way when we were expecting our first child.

How much I am looking forward to another great-grandchild.

Tuesday — February 5

Robert Benchley passed away in 1945 but stories about this humorous man live on.

Once when he was younger, he was visiting at the estate of a very elderly, boring, maiden aunt.

The dear old lady had planned to go for a walk with him after tea one afternoon but Benchley excused himself on account of bad weather.

Some time later his aunt found him going out the back alone.

"Oh Robert," she called, "has it cleared up?"

"Only partly," replied Benchley. "Enough for one but not enough for two."

Wednesday — February 6

Birds at Winter Nightfall

Around the house the flakes fly faster,
And all the berries now are gone
From holly and cotonea-aster
Around the house. The flakes fly! — faster
Shutting indoors that crumb-outcaster
We used to see upon the lawn
Around the house. The flakes fly faster,
And all the berries now are gone!

— *Thomas Hardy*

Thursday — February 7

Jake Frampton stopped by for dinner the other evening and we got into quite a lively discussion concerning funeral plots.

Although Jake is not "planning on leaving soon," as he put it, he felt that it would be wise to purchase some land at our local cemetery. As there are many plots available Jake was trying to decide where he would like to have his own.

The discussion prompted me to read to him Clarence Day's writing of his father's purchase, found in *Life with Father*:

> Father declared he was going to buy a new plot in the cemetery, a plot all for himself. "And I'll buy one on a corner," he added triumphantly, "where I can get out!"
>
> Mother looked at him, startled but admiring, and whispered to me, "I almost believe he could do it."

Jake decided that he hadn't thought of that at all but that he also might look for an available corner — just in case.

Friday — February 8

Do you remember when a juvenile delinquent was a youngster who owed six cents on an overdue library book?

Saturday — February 9

The other day I was reading a story in the newspaper, about two young boys from the United States who were here in Canada playing in a hockey tournament. This, of course, is not unusual; nor is it unusual when our boys go south of the border to play away from home against their American counterparts.

What interested me about these two boys was the fact that they play for teams in different cities, even though they are brothers. I was horrified to learn that their father rented an apartment in a city some hundred and fifty miles away for his wife and younger son so that this nine year old boy would get "better coaching."

This young lad's father saw nothing strange in splitting up his family for the hockey season. He and the older boy live and play hockey in one city; his wife and younger son live and play hockey one hundred and fifty miles away. They all see each other "when the break in the schedules permits."

This man insists that it is perfectly normal to want the best coaching for his sons.

I must confess that I find this to be a most abnormal situation. Am I simply old-fashioned in my thinking?

SUNDAY — FEBRUARY 10

GOETHE, who possessed a brilliant mind, wrote the following nine essentials to a full and contented life.

Health enough to make work a pleasure. Wealth enough to support your needs. Strength to battle with difficulties and overcome them. Grace enough to confess your sins and forsake them. Patience enough to toil until some good is accomplished. Charity enough to see some good in your neighbour. Love enough to move you to be useful and helpful to others. Faith enough to make real the things of God. Hope enough to remove all anxious fears concerning the future.

MONDAY — FEBRUARY 11

HAPPY the man who observes the heavenly and the terrestrial law in just proportion; whose every faculty, from the soles of his feet to the crown of his head, obeys the law of its level; who neither stoops nor goes on tiptoe, but lives a balanced life, acceptable to nature and God.

— *Henry David Thoreau*

Tuesday — February 12

TODAY is the birthday of Abraham Lincoln, one of the greatest American presidents. "I do the very best I know how; the very best I can; and I mean to keep on doing it to the end. If the end brings me out all right, what is said against me will not amount to anything. If the end brings me out all wrong, then a legion of angels swearing I was right will make no difference."

— *Abraham Lincoln*

Wednesday — February 13

ISN'T it amazing that we spend the first half of our lives accumulating things and the second half of our lives wondering what to do with all of them.

Thursday — February 14

HOW nice it is to have a special day to celebrate in the middle of the dreary winter months.

It is a special day for us to say, to those who are dear to us, how much we love them. Wouldn't it be even nicer to say "I love you" in word and by deed each and every day?

FRIDAY — FEBRUARY 15

RINGS and jewels are not gifts, but apologies for gifts. The only true gift is a portion of thyself.

— *Emerson*

SATURDAY — FEBRUARY 16

A handful of patience is worth more than a bushel of brains.

SUNDAY — FEBRUARY 17

O Lord, who hast taught that all our doings without love are nothing worth: send thy holy spirit and pour into our hearts that most excellent gift of love, the very bond of peace and of all virtues, without which whosoever liveth is counted dead before thee; Grant this for thine only son, Jesus Christ's sake. Amen.

— *Book of Common Prayer*

Monday — February 18

My grandson, Marshall, has taken up the sport of downhill skiing. Although he did some skiing as a young man it seemed that his studies took so much time that he really never became very proficient in the sport.

Now he has decided to make up for lost time. After a trip to a downtown sporting goods store, where he outfitted himself head to toe with ski-suit, hat, gloves, skis, boots, and poles, he dropped in to model his outfit for me.

As someone who was used to looking at voluminous ski wear, I was surprised to see how smart looking and lightweight the clothing and equipment has become. The ski boots and the fibreglass skis are a far cry from the old outfits that my husband George and I used to wear.

Marshall and his friends now ski at a private club near the town of Collingwood by Georgian Bay, Ontario. He and his chums have invited me to come and spend a day at their clubhouse, to sit by the fire and watch them all ski by.

I told them that if I didn't feel that they were doing well that I would strap on my old boards and give lessons!

Tuesday — February 19

As far back as I can remember, the Tuesday evening before Ash Wednesday has been the time for a "Pancake Social." In our early days of parish life, when Lent was more carefully observed, the evening would be our last social activity until after Easter.

The pancakes were usually prepared and served by the men of the parish. One of my favourite snapshots of George shows him with his black shirtsleeves rolled up, pancake flour dusting his cheek and a chef's hat at a rakish angle as he flipped pancakes on the huge griddle in the church kitchen.

It was always a very festive evening.

Tonight Bruce, Marg, and I joined the crowd at our church and enjoyed the same wonderful meal with about one hundred other members of our parish.

Our minister had obviously been practising his "flipping" at home, for, much to the delight of the youngsters present, he was able to flip the pancakes almost to the ceiling and catch them again.

Tonight was a most enjoyable time for young and old alike. It is pleasing to see a continuation of very old traditions of the church.

Wednesday — February 20

Ash Wednesday

In his ministry my husband George always emphasized the positive side of Lent; he saw it as a time of spiritual growth. I try to follow his idea and each Lenten time I choose a theme or one book of the Bible to read and reflect upon. Last year two of my neighbours joined me every Wednesday afternoon and this year there will be five of us to grow together.

Thursday — February 21

My good friends Will and Muriel are spending some time in the sunny south this year. Muriel wrote me this little story that I hope you find as amusing as I did.

"Last week several men in our community stopped in to ask Will to join the volunteer fire brigade. Will said that as he was a volunteer at home he would like very much to join. He also told them that he felt that because of his age he wouldn't do too well lifting or climbing ladders.

"That's all right," one of the gentlemen told him. "Usually by the time we get there, there's nothing left to lean a ladder on anyway."

FRIDAY — FEBRUARY 22

SARA Teasdale wrote this beautiful little poem called "February Twilight."

I stood beside a hill
Smooth with new-laid snow,
A single star looked out
From the cold evening glow.

There was no other creature
That saw what I could see —
I stood and watched the evening star
As long as it watched me.

SATURDAY — FEBRUARY 23

KNOWLEDGE and understanding are life's faithful companions who will never prove untrue to you. For knowledge is your crown and understanding your staff; and when they are with you, you can possess no greater treasures.

— *Kahlil Gibran*

SUNDAY — FEBRUARY 24

JESUS said, "Come unto me, all ye that labour and are heavy laden, and I will give you rest."

— *Matthew 11:28*

Monday — February 25

YOUNG John, my little next door neighbour, came over this afternoon with several of his young friends.

Marg, who still has some diet soda left from Bruce's slimming days, asked if they would like a drink.

All of the boys watched as she poured the pop into glasses for each of them.

John and his friends each thanked her politely and then John turned to his buddies and said, "I wonder which one of us got the calorie?"

Tuesday — February 26

MY friends Bernie and Elizabeth McNeill live on the coast in British Columbia along with most of their family.

Their son and his wife and family have moved east to Nova Scotia, however, and Elizabeth wrote to tell me of their granddaughter's last evening in B.C.

"Jill said her prayers, as she does each night, but as she finished she said, 'Well, God, it's goodbye forever tonight. Tomorrow we are moving to Nova Scotia.'!"

Wednesday — February 27

A man who deals in sunshine is the man who wins the crowds. He does a lot more business than the man who peddles clouds.

Thursday — February 28

As the month of February ends I must confess that I am pleased to see the end of a winter month and the beginning, tomorrow, of a spring month.

It isn't that I am ungrateful for the February days but as I move on in years I find that I feel the cold more each winter. I seem to add several more layers of clothing to keep out the winter's chill and, if nothing else, the weight of the added sweater or extra socks seems to bog me down.

Bruce suggested jokingly that I buy "electric socks," but he may just have a good idea there.

March

FRIDAY — MARCH 1

St. David's Day

ONE of the fondest memories of our trip to the British Isles many years ago is of our visit to the Cathedral of St. David's on the southwest coast of Wales.

It was late afternoon and the sun was shining through the beautiful stained glass windows where it reflected from the purple-grey stone of the sanctuary. The simplicity of the sanctuary was offset by two magnificent arrangements of large purple thistles. This whole setting seemed to typify the character of the Welsh people — the strength of granite, a touch of prickliness, and great charm.

We loved Wales and St. David's in particular.

SATURDAY — MARCH 2

MY husband George had a wonderful sense of humour and a smile was never far from his lips. I think that the first thing that drew me to him was his marvellous laugh. It seemed to start down near his toes and roll up, gathering strength and volume.

I have gathered several peoples' ideas of laughter for you to enjoy.

Laughing is the sensation of feeling good all over, and showing it principally in one spot.
— *Josh Billings*

Nothing shows a man's character more than what he laughs at.
— *Goethe*

When the world laughs at you, laugh back; it's just as funny as you are.

A laugh is a smile that burst.
— *John Donovan*

We are all here for a spell, get all the good laughs you can.
— *Will Rogers*

Sunday — March 3

JESUS said, "I am come that they might have life, and that they might have it more abundantly."

— *John 10:10*

Monday — March 4

AS you know, reading is one of my greatest pleasures. Although I enjoy reading many types of books I think that my favourite readings are those that are humorous. There is great pleasure in being able to see something in the same humorous way as the author, and in having a good chuckle as I am reading.

One of the authors whose books I have enjoyed reading more than any in the past few years is James Herriot, the British veterinarian.

His books recount the stories of his early professional life. The old farming characters, early and primitive drugs, and working conditions all form the basis of his hilarious stories.

For any of you that enjoy a good "belly-laugh" I heartily recommend the Herriot books!

Tuesday — March 5

The best gifts are tied with heart strings.

Wednesday — March 6

If a lass or a lad,
Simply has to be bad,
Because of compulsions inner,
Let it not be at school
Where the little fool
Would spoil the poor teacher's dinner.

Let it likewise not be
Where the neighbours can see
When objects are hurled and broken,
Or at church where the ear
Of the Preacher can hear
The horrible words that are spoken.

If a child must rage
At a certain age,
With hostile emotions a-tingle,
It's best that he foam
And explode at home,
Says the expert, who's probably single.

Thursday — March 7

Joy is not in things, it is in us.

Friday — March 8

The word *enthusiasm* is defined in the dictionary as "intense and passionate zeal." I can think of very little that is more important to people in this life than for them to have enthusiasm.

Here are a few lines from other writers about enthusiasm.

Nothing great was ever achieved without enthusiasm.

— Ralph Waldo Emerson

The best tool for any job — enthusiasm — makes heavy work lighter.

Enthusiasm is the most beautiful word on earth.

— Christian Morgenstern

Enthusiasm is the most convincing orator; it is like the infallible law of nature. The simplest man, fired with enthusiasm, is more persuasive than the most eloquent man without it.

SATURDAY — MARCH 9

JAKE told me an interesting story this morning about an American friend of his who was running for political office.

It was a rainy Friday evening and his friend was reading the paper in peace and comfort in front of the fire.

A knock came at his front door and when he opened it he saw a total stranger standing there.

"My car seems to have a dead battery and I was wondering if you could help me," said the damp gentleman.

"Why of course," said Jake's friend. "I have jumper cables. I'll just get my coat and we'll drive you to get your car."

He threw his cables into the back seat and drove the two blocks in a downpour to where the stranger's car was parked.

To his surprise the stranger got into his car and started it immediately.

"I didn't know anything about you," he said, "but anyone who would go to the trouble that you did to help a stranger this evening deserves my vote. I intend to tell my friends about this, as well, and I hope that they will vote for you too."

Jake's friend was elected and no doubt he will do as kind a job in his political office as he did on that rainy evening.

SUNDAY — MARCH 10

JESUS said, "Verily I say unto you, Inasmuch as ye have done it unto the least of these my brethren, ye have done it unto me."

— *Matthew 25:40*

MONDAY — MARCH 11

MY granddaughter Phyllis is a school teacher. From time to time she assigns special projects to groups of her young students. This term she allowed the children to divide themselves into working groups and to choose their own topics to work on.

The groups seemed to be getting organized pretty well and Phyllis was making notes on the topics chosen.

When she came to Tommy she inquired as to what their group was studying. Tommy told Phyllis proudly that his group was preparing to study and report on the condition of the world.

"My heavens," said Phyllis, "isn't that a little too difficult for the fourth grade?"

"Heck no," said Tommy. "There are five of us working on it, ma'am."

TUESDAY — MARCH 12

SOCIAL tact is making your company feel at home — even though you wish they were.

Wednesday — March 13

As my former readers know, I have been taking university courses for over a year now.

This year, much to everyone's surprise, I am taking computer science. Although I will have very few, if any, places to use the knowledge I am acquiring, I believe that it is important that I understand the computer.

The computer is one of the most important technological advances made by man, and its uses are almost limitless.

My grandchildren and great-grandchildren are all conversant with computers of all types and in order for me to be able to have discussions with them on related topics I, of course, must understand the computer.

At first I felt overwhelmed when I realized what computer science entailed. However, with the patient tutoring of my professor and my knowledgeable relatives I have become able to understand and use the computer.

If you think that "old dogs can't learn new tricks" perhaps you should give the computer a try. I'm sure that you will find it as absorbing as I have for the last few months.

Thursday — March 14

My father was a tremendous fan of jazz music and probably his favourite jazz musician was Louis Armstrong.

Daniel Louis Armstrong was born on July 4, 1900 in New Orleans. As a youth in the "city of jazz" he grew up loving the music for which the city was famous.

He spent several years playing on riverboats on the Mississippi River. He then joined up with "King" Oliver and they moved to Chicago in 1922.

Under Oliver's tutelage he went on to become the best-known and best-loved figure in jazz. "Satchmo," as he was nicknamed, represented the epitome of technical mastery and improvisation.

Armstrong made several European tours in the 50s and 60s and was a marvellous goodwill ambassador for the United States.

Although he passed away in 1971 he will long be remembered by all who love jazz.

Friday — March 15

Faith. You can do very little with it, but you can do nothing without it.

— *Samuel Butler*

Saturday — March 16

MARY McConnell was in a great state of excitement when she stopped by for tea today.

It seems that she won ten thousand dollars in a lottery draw the other evening.

"Edna, I can scarcely believe it! You know that I buy one ticket each week, just as I have for years, and I have never won as much as a nickel. This has come as such a surprise!"

Mary and her husband have ten children, an extraordinary family in this day and age, and the whole group has been discussing for two days now what should be done with the money. I am anxious to hear what their decision will be.

Sunday — March 17

St. Patrick's Day

THERE is an ancient hymn that is attributed to St. Patrick, who lived in the fourth century. It speaks of the strength of his faith.

I bind unto myself the name,
The strong name of the Trinity,
by invocation of the same
The three in one and one in three
of whom all nature has creation
eternal Father, Spirit, Word
Praise to the Lord of my salvation
Salvation is of Christ the Lord.

Monday — March 18

Our family has always enjoyed music very much. Although we don't all have the same musical ability we seem to have, at least, a great interest in music of many types.

Horace Walpole, who lived in the eighteenth century, wrote this about music.

"Had I children, my utmost endeavors should be to make them musicians. Considering I have no ear, nor even thought of music, the preference seems odd, and yet it is embraced on frequent recollection. In short, as my aim would be to make them happy, I think it the most probable method. It is a resource which will last them their lives, unless they grow deaf; it depends upon themselves, not on others; always amuses and soothes, if not consoles; and of all fashionable pleasures, is the cheapest."

Tuesday — March 19

Don't cling to the old because it made you glad once: go on to the next, the next region, the next experience.

— *Alfred North Whitehead*

Wednesday — March 20

As we grow older a major concern to many of us is whether or not we will need more care than our family is able to give us. I refer of course to our possible need to live in retirement or nursing homes.

I would like to tell you about my friend Edna Jones and her experience.

Edna and her husband Ernie lived much of their lives in Cowansville in the province of Quebec. They had four sons and were very involved with them in sports. They were leaders in the life in their community.

When Ernie retired they moved to an apartment in Kitchener, Ontario to be closer to their sons.

Time passed and Ernie's health deteriorated. He was moved into a nursing home and every day Edna would take the bus from her apartment to the home to visit him.

Eventually Ernie passed away. Shortly thereafter, Edna's sons felt that she was becoming forgetful and that a retirement home was now necessary for her.

Edna moved into the home but for the first six months was quite resentful and unhappy. Fortunately her determined nature and usual cheeriness returned. She once again became involved, running exercise classes for her neighbours, organizing bridge clubs, and getting everyone involved in really living again.

I salute Edna Jones today.

Thursday — March 21

This cheerful little German folk poem expresses my pleasure at the coming of spring.

All the birds have come again,
Hear the happy chorus!
Robin, bluebird, on the wing,
Thrush and wren this message bring
Spring will soon come marching in,
Come with joyous singing.

Friday — March 22

Be, Lord, within me to strengthen me, without me to preserve, over me to shelter, beneath me to support, before me to direct, behind me to bring back, round about me to fortify.

— *Lancelot Andrews*

Saturday — March 23

The first rule of wise financial management is to save something for a rainy day; the second, to distinguish between light sprinkles and heavy showers.

Sunday — March 24

Jesus said unto his disciples, "If any man will come after me, let him deny himself, and take up his cross, and follow me."

— *Matthew 16:24*

Monday — March 25

Mary McConnell came by today to tell me about the decisions that she and her family have made about their prize money.

"Instead of rushing out to spend the money, we have come up with what we thought would be the best investment we could make — the children's future.

"The money has been invested in ten, one thousand dollar term deposits. As you know, Edna, with ten children it sometimes gets to be difficult to save much for university. Each child now has the first one thousand dollars toward post secondary education. If any one of them decides not to go to university the thousand dollars is theirs to invest, at that time, in whatever they wish." I couldn't think of a better way to invest the winnings!

Tuesday — March 26

The supreme end of education is expert discernment in all things — the power to tell the good from the bad, the genuine from the counterfeit, and to prefer the good and the genuine to the bad and the counterfeit.

— *Samuel Johnson*

Wednesday — March 27

I had a delightful phone call from my great-grandson Geoffrey last evening. He was quite excited as he talked about his marvellous new bird feeder. He made his feeder at school in his shop class and he and his dad erected it in the back yard.

"This morning there was a cardinal feeding, Gram, and at lunchtime we saw a whole lot of chickadees eating and making a terrific mess." His voice went up even more in his excitement. "Then guess what, Grammie! Tonight we saw a blue jay and when he arrived all the others left; he was just like a "king in the castle."

Thursday — March 28

Men of thought should have nothing to do with action.

— *Oscar Wilde*

Friday — March 29

As anyone who has a pet knows, the attachments that form between pets and owners can be as strong as feelings for fellow humans.

Pets place no value on our station in life, our wealth, or our lack of it. They care not a whit whether our home is large or small.

What matters to them is the love and affection that they are shown. A pet, treated well, gives loyalty that would put many people to shame.

This love from our animals can help to alleviate any loneliness we may feel.

With this in mind many nursing and retirement homes have dropped their old codes of "sterility above all" and are allowing the elderly to bring dogs and cats with them into their new dwellings.

Nurses and doctors alike are thrilled to see the new interest that many elderly people show when a small kitten is placed in their care. People who have previously shown little interest in anything seem to come to life when given an animal as a responsibility.

A little love goes a very long way.

Saturday — March 30

All my life I have been an early riser and, as often as not, I will be up to have a cup of tea before six a.m. In winter months it is still pitch black at that hour but now as the days grow longer it is lighter much earlier.

I like to sit at my window watching the new day unfold.

The odd bird comes to light on the feeder, scattering seedshells with gay abandon.

Young John, our neighbour, whistles, his breath visible in icy fingers, as he delivers the morning papers.

It's nice to see the world gradually pick up its pace until somewhere around eight thirty the hectic bustle of another day begins.

Sunday — March 31

Palm Sunday

Jesus said, "Whosoever will be chief among you, let him be your servant. Even as the Son of man came not to be ministered unto, but to minister, and to give his life a ransom for many."

— *Mark 10:44–45*

April

MONDAY — APRIL 1

AFTER years of experience I have learned to pray to God not for what I wish, but for what I deserve.

TUESDAY — APRIL 2

THE year's at the spring,
And day's at the morn,
Morning's at seven;
The hillside's dew-pearled;
The lark's on the wing;
The snail's on the thorn:
God's in His Heaven —
All's right with the world.

— *Robert Browning*

Wednesday — April 3

My daughter Mary and her husband John are moving again. I am thankful that it is really a very short-term move this time because this time they are going to the far north.

For the next six months John and Mary will be living in a small town near Yellowknife in the Northwest Territories.

Mary is very pleased with this upcoming change. She spent many years travelling with John and the children to far distant places — Korea, Africa, and the Middle East. Some people might have found these moves difficult because the language and customs are all different. Mary and John seemed to revel in it. The challenge of learning new languages and customs seemed only to increase their enjoyment of each new place.

John will be spending time with the bishop in the N.W.T. setting up new programs for the native children in the area.

Mary plans to see as much as she can and learn of the customs of Canadians that she has never met.

Fortunately they will not have to sell their home here. As John says, "It seems just like an interesting six month vacation."

THURSDAY — APRIL 4

PHYLLIS told me this story of a pupil in her friend Christie's class.

The children were drawing industriously when Christie approached a little girl who was really putting her heart and soul into her efforts. "Who is that you're drawing?" asked Christie.

"It's God," the little girl replied.

"But Kelly, nobody knows what God looks like."

"Well, they will when I get finished," Kelly replied brightly.

FRIDAY — APRIL 5

Good Friday

JESUS said, "Father, forgive them; for they know not what they do."

— *Luke 23:34*

SATURDAY — APRIL 6

MEMORY is the only paradise from which we cannot be driven.

— *Jean Paul Richter*

Sunday — April 7

Easter

JESUS said, "I am the resurrection and the life: he that believeth in me, though he were dead, yet shall he live.

And whosoever liveth and believeth in me shall never die. Believest thou this?"

— *John 11:25*

Monday — April 8

THE month of April is such a beautiful time. The birds are returning from the south, the buds on the trees are beginning to open, and the crocuses are pushing up through the earth.

Mrs. McGuiness and I went for a lovely long walk today. It was so wonderful to see and smell the new growth.

When you are in the latter portion of your life, you are always grateful for the opportunity of welcoming a new season — at least that is how I feel about it today.

There is a happy optimism about this new period of the year beginning. It is much as each new segment of our lives unfolds — bright and new.

Both Mrs. McGuiness and I returned from our walk rejuvenated and in great spirits.

Tuesday — April 9

There are two times in a man's life when he should not speculate: when he can't afford it and when he can.

— *Mark Twain*

Wednesday — April 10

Today is the anniversary of the original Arbor Day, celebrated back in 1872 in Nebraska.

Oliver Wendell Holmes expressed a very lovely thought on tree planting.

"It is something to make two blades of grass grow where only one was growing, it is much more to have been the occasion of the planting of an oak which shall defy twenty scores of winters, or of an elm which shall canopy with its green cloud of foliage half as many generations of mortal immortalities."

Thursday — April 11

It is great to have friends when one is young, but it is still more so when you are getting old. When we are young, friends are, like everything else, a matter of course. In our old days we know what it means to have them.

— *Edward Grieg*

Friday — April 12

There are incidents in our lives that stand out like beacons — marriages, births, deaths.

And then there are the other occasions that are truly unforgettable — the embarrassing moments.

The first time that comes to my mind was the day that I punched Bill Green in the nose so hard that his nose bled.

There I was, daughter of the minister, knuckles bruised, standing in the corner of our one-room school house awaiting the arrival of my father, who had been summoned by our teacher. I shall never forget the feeling of absolute mortification as I stood, trying not to cry, awaiting my fate.

I will also never forget the time that, as a young minister's wife, I managed to dump an entire pot of tea down the front of a visiting bishop.

Fortunately the passage of time usually turns these ghastly experiences into amusing stories. I often have to remind myself of that fact.

Saturday — April 13

Freedom is the right to be wrong, not the right to do wrong.

— *John Diefenbaker*

Sunday — April 14

Jesus came and stood in their midst, and saith unto them, "Peace be unto you." And when he had so said, he showed unto them his hands and his side. Then were the disciples glad, when they saw the Lord.

Then Jesus said unto them again, "Peace be unto you: as my Father has sent me, even so send I you."

— *John 20:19–21*

Monday — April 15

Chief Seattle, chief of the Suquamish Indian tribe, for whom the city of Seattle is named, said:

"What is man without the beasts? If all the beasts were gone, man would die from great loneliness of spirit, for whatever happens to the beasts also happens to man. All things are connected."

Tuesday — April 16

April, April,
Laugh thy girlish laughter;
Then, the moment after,
Weep thy girlish tears!
April, that mine ears
Like a lover greetest,
If I tell thee, sweetest,
All my hopes and fears,
April, April,
Laugh thy golden laughter,
But, the moment after,
Weep thy golden tears!

— *William Watson*

Wednesday — April 17

Marg and Bruce are floating on the clouds tonight. Their daughter Phyllis has just called to say that during her doctor's visit this afternoon he detected *two* heart beats. We are going to have twins in our family!

"It is just like Phyllis to do this, isn't it Edna?" Bruce remarked. "Even as a child, she wanted to do things better than anyone else, and that stubborn streak in her usually enabled her to succeed."

I'm sure that Phyllis and Bill are delighted at being doubly-blessed. May God grant them the joy of a healthy birth.

THURSDAY — APRIL 18

BRUCE'S way of showing his excitement over yesterday's great news is to have a burst of energy that will give us a clean garage in the next few hours.

Since quite early this morning he has been crashing and banging outside, doing "a little straightening" as he put it.

In actual fact I believe he has stripped the garage bare in his zeal, for as I look out the window the entire driveway and front yard seem to be buried.

He did manage to find the old pine cradle that has been in our family for generations. My own mother rocked me as an infant, and I, in turn, rocked our daughters in this beautiful old cradle.

Bruce is very handy with wood and he now plans to make a second little bed for Phyllis and Bill to put in the babies' nursery.

Several of the neighbours thought that Bruce was having a garage sale and were busy looking at all the items in the yard.

He laughed as he told them that this was, in fact, a cleaning that the garage was getting, not a clearing out.

I think that Marg is rather hoping this burst of enthusiasm will lead to clean windows later in the day.

FRIDAY — APRIL 19

THE headline of a recent magazine article said, "Come on senior citizens. Forget armchair travelling and discover that this is the best time to see the world."

How right that is! If you think about it, we seniors have a definite advantage over junior travellers.

The first and foremost advantage is our flexibility. We have the freedom to travel at times when many others cannot. Travelling just before or just after peak seasons usually means substantial savings on transportation, food, and lodging. This flexibility also allows us to take advantage of special promotion-priced travel plans with special time requirements.

Another advantage that results in economizing on travel expenditures is the senior citizen discount offered both here and abroad. To be able to use this discount it is usually necessary to have proof of age; your passport will do.

It is wise to remember that half the fun of any trip is the preparation for it. Studying the sights you'd like to see and the areas you've arranged to visit makes travel more rewarding.

The next time you sit in that armchair maybe you'll be recounting your own trips with travel tales and photographs.

Saturday — April 20

My dear friend Marcia sent me this amusing story of an American student studying at Oxford University in England.

This lad was studying a special course leading to an important examination. His professor suggested that he attend a series of twelve lectures on the course.

The professor noted his presence in the first of the lectures. In the following eleven the American was conspicuously absent.

The professor saw him on campus on occasion, but made no comment, as he felt the examination would give the student his due.

To the professor's chagrin the American passed with a mark of ninety five percent!

When the professor next saw the student he said, "I cannot understand your mark seeing that you cut all but the first of my lectures."

"Well," said the American, "I guess I should have scored one hundred percent. The only way that I can figure it is that your first lecture got me confused."

Sunday — April 21

Jesus said, "I am the good shepherd: the good shepherd giveth his life for the sheep."

— *John 10:11*.

Monday — April 22

Here Lies
Ezekial Aikle
Aged 102
The Good
Die Young

This epitaph is on a tombstone in Nova Scotia. What a wonderful tribute.

Tuesday — April 23

St. George, the patron saint of England, has long been one of my favourite "folk" heroes. Little is known of his life and martyrdom, which now is lost in the mists of history.

Yet this "Soldier of Goodness" has been a symbol of courage and dedication for centuries in English culture. Today's celebration is one way of keeping alive the virtues associated with St. George.

Wednesday — April 24

All ambitions are lawful except those which climb upward on the miseries or credulities of mankind.

— *Joseph Conrad*

Thursday — April 25

The last few years have seen tremendous advances made by women in every field.

There are women in virtually all areas — more women are doctors, corporate executives, labourers, and so on.

Ontario had Pauline McGibbon as its lieutenant governor; Britain has had Margaret Thatcher as its prime minister; the United States had Sally Ride as its first woman astronaut aboard the space shuttle.

All of these accomplishments are wonderful.

What causes me some anxiety, however, is the group of women who choose to stay in the home and raise their family.

The attitude today seems to minimize the contribution these women make to society. I feel that an injustice is done when a woman is made to feel guilty for wanting to be home as a mother and homemaker instead of wanting to join the workforce.

What job could be more important than that of guiding our future generations?

Many women have to work in order to provide for their families. This is important, and these women deserve our support and encouragement.

It is also important that we support homemakers in their vital role.

FRIDAY — APRIL 26

NO man is born into the world whose work
is not born with him; there is always work
and tools to work withal, for those who will;
And blessed are the horny hands of toil;
The busy world shoves angrily aside
The man who stands with arms akimbo set,
Until occasion tells him what to do;
And he who waits to have his task marked out,
Shall die and leave his errand unfulfilled.

— *James Russell Lowell*

SATURDAY — APRIL 27

REMEMBER that you ought to behave in life as you would at a banquet. As something is being passed around it comes to you; stretch out your hand, take a portion of it politely. It passes on; do not detain it. Or it has not come to you yet; do not project your desire to meet it, but wait until it comes in front of you.

This interesting analogy was written, not recently, as I had imagined, but in the year 60 A.D. by Epictetus. It's hard to believe that advice that is so pertinent today could have been written over two thousand years ago.

Sunday — April 28

We thank you, God, for soft green grass
and budding leaves,
For simple music of the wind
through swaying trees,
We thank you, God, for quiet nights and stars
that shine,
For order in this universe of your design.

— *Frances Hill West*

Monday — April 29

If we had no faults we should not take so much pleasure in noting those of others.

— *de la Rochefoucauld*

Tuesday — April 30

Don't part with your illusions. When they have gone, you may still exist, but you have ceased to live.

May

WEDNESDAY — MAY 1

A delicate fabric of bird song
Floats in the air,
The smell of wet wild earth
Is everywhere.

Red small leaves of the maple
Are clenched like a hand,
Like girls at their first communion
The pear trees stand.

Oh I must pass nothing by
Without loving it much,
The raindrop try with my lips,
The grass with my touch;

For how can I be sure
I shall see again
The world, on the first of May,
Shining after the rain.

— *Sara Teasdale*

THURSDAY — MAY 2

MY friend Emily has returned to her home in Philadelphia after her winter sojourn in Florida.

Emily travels often and, in doing so, has many occasions to eat in restaurants.

"You know, Edna," she wrote in her last letter, "I eat out very regularly but I confess that my favourite restaurants are in Florida.

"The restaurant owners in this state seem to have a rather unique idea that I don't believe I have seen elsewhere. This idea is called 'Early Bird Dinners.'

"It is designed to suit people who like to eat at an early hour, such as five, rather than the more elegant times of seven or eight o'clock.

"The 'Early Bird' dinners are usually served at a more reasonable price, as well, thus making restaurants more accessible to those on a lower income.

"As a senior I really appreciate this. Most of my friends and I like to eat an early dinner anyway, and the discount in prices enables us to eat out more often.

"I'm sure the restauranteurs have adapted this plan to suit the many retirees that live here in Florida, but wouldn't it be nice to find 'Early Bird Dinners' in other areas as well?"

FRIDAY — MAY 3

NO man knows his true character until he has run out of gas, purchased something on the installment plan, and raised an adolescent.

SATURDAY — MAY 4

LEARN from the mistakes of others. You can't live long enough to make them all yourself.

SUNDAY — MAY 5

O praise God in his sanctuary, praise him in the firmament of his power.
Praise him in his mighty acts, praise him according to his excellent greatness.
Praise him in the sound of the trumpet, praise him upon the lute and harp.
Let everything that hath breath praise the Lord.

— *Psalm 150*

MONDAY — MAY 6

NOTHING is worth more than this day.

— *Goethe*

TUESDAY — MAY 7

EXPERIENCE is probably the greatest teacher. A child may read about the ocean but until he has seen its vastness or the majesty of its waves or experienced the feel of the salt water on his skin he really cannot understand the ocean.

It is the same in all things. So many writers have expressed thoughts on experience and here are but a few.

Experience is the name everyone gives to their mistakes.

— *Oscar Wilde*

Experience is the comb that nature gives us when we are bald.

— *Belgian proverb*

Life is a series of experiences, each one of which makes us bigger, even though it is sometimes hard to realize this.

— *Henry Ford*

We learn from experience. A man never wakes up his second baby just to see it smile.

— *Grace Williams*

We are not sure whether age comes with experience or experience with age.

WEDNESDAY — MAY 8

THE other day Jake told me about an interesting publishing venture that took place in Toronto. A group of residents in a senior citizens' home worked together to publish a collection of poems, vignettes, and true stories, together with illustrations, that would be a record of their collective memories. Since the average age of the residents was 86, this history would span nearly a century!

These energetic men and women successfully overcame the many practical problems associated with the publishing business, and at the same time managed to write their own contributions. The result is a delightful and very professional-looking book that is full of wonderful stories about people and places of long ago. In fact, one week after its publication, *The Past is Precious* was completely sold out!

What a loss to us all if these memories had been allowed simply to disappear. And what an example to those of us who are also senior citizens. We don't have to sit on the sidelines just because we are older. There is much we can do that is worthwhile and enjoyable.

Thursday — May 9

WILL Hampton has a marvellous green thumb. He has an extraordinary way of making his plants and flowers grow well, and his skill at the garden's layout is rivalled by none.

Will dropped over today to discuss with Marg and me our planting for this year's garden in the yard.

As we walked through the yard Will was able to tell us which blooms would look best where and which needed more sun or shade. I'm sure we will enjoy our garden this year more than we ever have.

Friday — May 10

The Cloud

I bring fresh showers for the thirsting flowers,
From the seas and the streams;
I bear light shade for the leaves when laid
In their noonday dreams.
From my wings are shaken the dews that
  waken
The sweet buds every one,
When rocked to rest on their mother's breast,
As she dances about the sun.
I wield the flail of the lashing hail,
And whiten the green plains under;
And then again I dissolve it in rain,
And laugh as I pass in thunder.

— *Percy Bysshe Shelley*

Saturday — May 11

In the spring nothing pleases me more than a drive into the countryside to see the farms.

"As a work of art, I know few things more pleasing to the eye, or more capable of affording scope and gratification to a taste for the beautiful, than a well-situated, well-cultivated farm."

Edward Everett made these remarks in Buffalo, New York in 1857 but I feel the same today more than one hundred years later.

Sunday — May 12

Mother's Day

In my lifetime, I have observed and experienced great changes in the role of women in the home and society. But one central role remains for a woman who is prepared to fulfill it, namely that of motherhood.

"One lamp — thy mother's love — amid the stars Shall lift its pure flame changeless, and before The throne of God, burn through eternity — Holy — as it was lit and lent thee here."

— *Nathaniel Parker Willis*

Monday — May 13

Phyllis and Bill dropped over yesterday for lunch. Although Phyllis is not expecting her babies for some time yet she certainly is getting to be quite a size.

Phyllis and Bill have always been careful in their eating habits and so there has been very little need to change what or when they eat. The only cravings that Phyllis experienced have been for fried clams! I told her that it comes from having family roots in the east coast.

Tuesday — May 14

The United States Navy Department is famous for its special sayings. Here is a directive on safety.

You're enjoying good health.
  That's fine.
You want to remain well.
  That's natural.
You may be careless.
  That's possible.
You may have an accident.
  That's probable.
You sincerely hope not.
  That's obvious.
Then practise safety first.
  That's wisdom.

Wednesday — May 15

It is possible that our race may be an accident, in a meaningless universe, living its brief life uncared-for, on this dark cooling star: but even so — and all the more — what marvellous creatures we are! What fairy story, what tale from the Arabian Nights of the jinns, is a hundredth part as wonderful as this true story of simians.

It is so much more heartening, too, than the tales we invent. A universe capable of giving birth to many such accidents is — blind or not — a good world to live in, a promising universe.

— *Clarence Day*

Thursday — May 16

The Ascension of Christ speaks to us of life beyond this world, as do Jesus' words in his sermon on the mount:

"Lay up for yourselves treasures in heaven, where neither moth nor rust doth corrupt, and where thieves do not break through nor steal; for where your treasure is, there will your heart be also."

— *Matthew 6:20–21*

Friday — May 17

We were talking this evening about schools and teachers. In trying to assess our ideas of what makes a good teacher I think that Jake made the most interesting comment when he said, "I think that the best that can be said of a teacher is 'He has had twenty years experience' not 'He has had one year's experience twenty times'!"

Saturday — May 18

A little nonsense now and then
Is relished by the wisest men.

— *Old proverb*

Sunday — May 19

Today, in church, we prayed for God's blessing on those who sow the seed.

"Almighty and most merciful God, from whom cometh every good and perfect gift, Bless we beseech thee, the labours of thy people and cause the earth to bring forth her fruits abundantly in their season, that we may with grateful hearts give thanks to thee for the same, through Jesus Christ our Lord.

— *Book of Common Prayer*

Monday — May 20

This third Monday of May has become our first spring holiday weekend. In my childhood, the holiday was kept on the actual birthday of Queen Victoria, May 24th. With the development of the automobile and extensive ownership of cottage property, longer weekends were desirable. To this end, the holiday was moved to the Monday preceeding the 24th.

This is usually the first of regular trips to the cottage. For home gardeners, it is the time for transplanting annuals and the setting out of vegetable plants.

Gardening is something I have always enjoyed. Starting and nurturing new life is as rewarding and pleasurable an activity as there is. From all the gardening supplies that I've seen for sale in the stores, I think that many people feel the same way that I do.

Tuesday — May 21

How is it that our memory is good enough to retain the least triviality that happens to us, and yet not good enough to recollect how often we have told it to the same person?

— *de la Rochefoucauld*

WEDNESDAY — MAY 22

I am not sure of the original source of this poem but it was sent to me by Laura and Robert, elderly friends of mine living in Alberta.

Age is a state of mind . . .
If you've left your dreams behind,
If hope is lost; if you no longer look ahead,
If your ambitious fires are dead —
Then you are old!

But if in life you hold the best
And if in life you keep the zest,
If love of God and man you hold
No matter how the years go by . . .
No matter how the birthdays fly —
You are not old!

THURSDAY — MAY 23

ARE you old enough to remember when they restricted what was in the movies, not what was in the audience?

FRIDAY — MAY 24

GOD Almighty first planted a garden; and, indeed, it is the purest of human pleasures.

— *Francis Bacon*

Saturday — May 25

UNTIL we have faced some great adversity in this life, it is hard to know how we will react.

I like to think that I would be able to handle misfortune with courage but until we are put to the test it is difficult to know.

I greatly admire the bravery in people who are, through some misfortune, forced to deal with difficult times.

One person of outstanding courage who comes to my mind is Jocelyn Lovell, the great Canadian cyclist.

Lovell was probably the best cyclist that Canada has ever had. He won many medals in events all over the globe.

Two years ago, Lovell had an accident while practising on a back road in Milton. The accident came very close to taking his life, but, while he was spared, he has been left a quadriplegic. How easy it would be to be bitter or angry!

Instead Jocelyn and his wife, former speed skater Sylvia Burka, are committed to finding Jocelyn's full potential and using it to benefit him and other similarly afflicted athletes. This is courage!

Sunday — May 26

For the work of the Spirit in the history of the world, through peaceful advance, through praise and tumult,

We thank Thee, O Lord.

For the work of the Spirit, within and beyond the bounds of thy visible Church,

We thank Thee, O Lord.

For all those who show forth Thy Spirit outside the circle of organized religion,

We thank Thee, O Lord.

For the work of Thy Spirit in the Church which will not cease until it has joined all nations and people into one family to Thy praise and glory,

We thank Thee, O Lord.

Monday — May 27

This day marks an American holiday, Memorial Day.

Bring the Flag and set it there,
Let it proudly wave in air
O'er the grassy hillock where
The sleeping heroes stay.

— *Abbie Farwell Brown*

TUESDAY — MAY 28

MY husband George was an excellent speaker. His sermons were well thought-out and delivered. Old Mr. Hardy one day asked George the secret of his success and George told him that it was this prayer that seemed to help him the most: "Lord, fill my mouth with worthwhile stuff, And nudge me when I've said enough."

WEDNESDAY — MAY 29

JAKE Frampton was in for tea today. Since it was such a lovely day we had tea in the yard. He was interested in the birds that are nesting in the big willow tree.

I enjoyed seeing the shoots of flowers that are growing so well in the warm sun.

I was reminded of the following:

"Five men went into the same field. The geologist found various rocks and their formations. The botanist saw many kinds of plants. The entomologist was excited to find beetles, butterflies, and other insects. The farmer found the good soil. The artist saw the waving branches of the tree against the blue sky. Five men, in the same field, and each found something different and each found what they were looking for."

Thursday — May 30

Perseverance wins over almost any obstacles. The person who is not willing to give up without "just one more" try is sure to come out on top eventually.

Think where we would be today if Thomas Edison had given up before finding a successful filament for the lightbulb, or if Alexander Graham Bell had not persisted with the telephone.

What if Dr. Salk had not found the polio vaccine, or if insulin from Banting and Best didn't exist?

Friday — May 31

I must confess that I find smoking an abhorrent vice. Too often smokers are careless with the ashes or the butts and there seems always to be a stale smoke odour about the homes of smokers.

For these reasons I particularly enjoyed this sign in a nearby restaurant.

"If you want to put your ashes and cigarette butts in your cup and saucer, let the waitress know and she will serve your coffee in an ashtray."

June

Saturday — June 1

My husband George and I shared a wonderful and happy marriage. Although we were both very young when we married, and George's salary was meagre, we seemed to be rich in so many other ways.

We enjoyed many close friendships, we had a wonderful family, and although money was scarce, good times were a-plenty.

I think this happiness is what enabled me to carry on after George's passing. I have had so many good things to remember that some days it is as if he is still here. His spirit and the spirit of our marriage really does live on.

Sunday — June 2

FATHER most holy, merciful and loving Jesus, redeemer, ever to be worshipped, Life-giving Spirit, comforter most gracious, God everlasting.

— *Hymn 489*

Monday — June 3

FEW people in this world work harder than the farmer. Their hours are long and much of the success of their crops depends upon the weather.

I particularly enjoyed this story of a farming friend of my sister Sarah.

A young doctor opened his practice in a rural area of New Brunswick. He was awakened on his second morning by the ring of his doorbell at 4:30 a.m. As he stumbled in the dark toward the door his mind was scrambling to be alert for what he assumed must be a terrible emergency. When he opened the door he was surprised to see a farmer, looking quite fit.

"Good Heavens, man, what is it?" asked the doctor urgently.

"Well, nothing much," said the farmer. "You asked me to drop by for my blood test just before breakfast, and here I am."

Tuesday — June 4

"Young men are fitter to invent than to judge; fitter for execution than for counsel, and fitter for new projects than for settled business."

— *Francis Bacon*

Wednesday — June 5

Several years ago a few enterprising young men came up with a new game, called Trivial Pursuit. It is a game that requires knowledge of an almost limitless number of interesting facts in areas such as geography, history, sports, etc.

I seem to be luckier than most when playing and I feel quite certain that a good deal of my luck comes not only from having a good memory for details, but also from the fact that I have been alive for more years than most of the people that I play with.

This game has become very popular in our family and rarely will a family get-together pass without someone challenging another to a game.

My husband George would have been a whiz at this game! His knowledge of trivial facts was truly amazing.

I thank the young gentlemen whose ideas have given us so many pleasurable hours.

Thursday — June 6

Look to your health; and if you have it, praise God and value it next to a good conscience; for health is the second blessing that we mortals are capable of — a blessing that money cannot buy.

— *Izaak Walton*

Friday — June 7

Some of the world's most notable personalities made major contributions to this life after they were 80. Just a few are named below with their accomplishments of later life.

At 91, Eamon DeValera served as president of Ireland.

At 90, Pablo Picasso was still producing drawings and engravings.

At 89, Arthur Rubinstein gave one of his greatest recitals at Carnegie Hall in New York.

At 88, Konrad Adenauer was the chancellor of Germany.

At 84, W. Somerset Maugham wrote *Points of View*.

At 81, Benjamin Franklin effected the compromise that led to the adoption of the U.S. constitution.

Truly amazing isn't it?

SATURDAY — JUNE 8

A young friend of Phyllis and Bill's recently suffered a nervous breakdown. We were all very upset by his illness; he is a young man with a wife and two small sons, and there seemed to be very little that we could do to help.

We talked about this problem a good deal within our family and several interesting points came up.

As Bill pointed out, "You know, this could have happened to any one of us, young or old. I don't believe that anyone knows what causes a breakdown or even the danger signals that could be warnings of something serious to come."

Fred's comments were also interesting. "The stress in our lives is so great today that many of us don't realize where our breaking point is. If we have jobs we are lucky, and often the concern of losing our jobs, particularly when we have families, can be overwhelming."

The most important thing now is to be of help to this young man while he is on the road to recovery. Because so little is understood, even in medical circles, about breakdowns the best that any of us can do is to be supportive, give ears to listen, shoulders to lean on, and love and understanding as he returns to good health and happiness.

SUNDAY — JUNE 9

SEEK ye first the kingdom of God, and His righteousness; and all these things shall be added unto you.

— *Matthew 6:33*

MONDAY — JUNE 10

YESTERDAY, as you may know, was my birthday and the whole family gathered here to help me celebrate.

Just before it was time to have the cake my daughter Julia presented me with an enormous gift-wrapped box.

Well, I took the wrapping off and dug my way through a mound of paper. Finally at the bottom of this gigantic box was an envelope, and in the envelope was a round trip ticket to London, England.

I could not have been more surprised! The girls had written to my friend Peggy Cay in England to find a suitable time for a visit. Peggy's letter was enclosed with the ticket and her letter brought tears to my eyes.

All it said was
"Dear Edna,
Anytime!
With love
Peggy."

Tuesday — June 11

The codfish lays a million eggs
While the faithful hen lays one,
But the codfish does not cackle
To inform us what she's done;
So we disregard the codfish,
While the faithful hen we prize,
While only goes to prove
It pays to advertise!

I never cease to be amazed at the power of advertising in our society. The addition of television to radio and newspapers has added a powerful dimension to advertising.

One of the most interesting promotions that I can remember happened near Christmas in 1983.

Homely dolls called "Cabbage Patch Kids" became "the doll" to ask for at Santa's knee.

The manufacturing company of the dolls had no way of anticipating the demand for these unusual looking dolls, and so they were soon in very short supply. In stores, people were literally fighting to get one or more dolls before Christmas.

I suppose this nonsense only gave stronger credence to the old adage, "It pays to advertise!"

Wednesday — June 12

I suppose that every old scholar has had the experience of reading something in a book which was significant to him, but which he could never find again. Sure he is that he read it there, but no one else ever read it, nor can he find it again, though he buy the book and ransack every page.

— *Ralph Waldo Emerson*

Thursday — June 13

As I sit outside in the evening, I enjoy watching the moon and the stars become clear in the darkening sky.

I still have great difficulty realizing that man has, indeed, walked on the moon.

The advances that man has made in the last eighty five years are truly mind-boggling.

I wonder if we will continue to advance with such enormous strides or whether we will enter a levelling-off period. I cannot imagine what the future holds in store if we continue to advance at such an incredible pace.

In many ways I feel it would be better for us all if we could slow down just a little and enjoy some of the fruits of our labours. It seems that we are losing some of the pleasures of relaxation in our tremendous efforts to keep up the pace.

Friday — June 14

Russia has abolished God, but so far God has been more tolerant.

Saturday — June 15

Some folks just don't seem to realize, when they're moaning about not getting their prayers answered, that NO is the answer.

Sunday — June 16

Father's Day

This is the day that we remember, with love, the first man in our lives.

Although my father passed away many years ago now, I am still appreciating his wonderful influence. You see, it was dad who nurtured our interest in books and reading.

"I just have something I want you to hear," he would say. He would then read selected passages, often from Mark Twain or other popular writers. He would choose a particularly humorous or interesting bit that would leave us spellbound or laughing uproariously.

"That bit was from *Tom Sawyer*," he would say casually, and the book would be left for us to grab for.

Books are a great part of my life and each time I pick a new one to read, my thoughts turn to my father who really got me started. I will be forever grateful to him.

Monday — June 17

Several years ago my granddaughter Phyllis found this seventeenth century writing, *Haec Mulier* ("This Woman").

We are as free-born as men, have as free election, and as free spirits. We are compounded of like parts, and may with like liberty make benefit of our creations: my countenance shall smile on the worthy and frown on the ignoble. I will hear the wise and be deaf to idiots; give counsel to my friends, but be dumb to flatterers. I have hands that shall be liberal to reward desert, feet that shall move swiftly to do good office, and thoughts that shall ever accompany freedom and severity.

Tuesday — June 18

If you have learned to walk
A little more sure-footedly than I,
Be patient with my stumbling then
And know that only as I do my best and try
May I attain the goal
For which we both are striving.

If through experience, your soul
Has gained heights which I
As yet in dim-lit vision see,
Hold out your hand and point the way
Lest from its straightness I should stray
And walk a mile with me.

Wednesday — June 19

Gordie Howe was a hockey player of incredible talent. Howe also had two sons who followed in his footsteps and played hockey in the National Hockey League. Anyone who followed hockey remembers Gordie playing on a line with his sons, an amazing feat.

Many people may not know, however, that the Howes had a son who chose a medical career rather than one in hockey. Gordie likes to tell the story of how Murray met his future wife.

At a social event Murray met a lovely young lady. She said to him, "My name is Colleen."

"My mother's name is Colleen," said Murray.

"Well, you'll never believe how I got my name. My father was a real hockey nut and there was some old guy named Gordie Howe who played hockey. If I had been a boy I was to be named Gordie, after him. As you can see I'm not, so instead, I was named for his wife, Colleen."

"Well," said Murray, "you're not going to believe my story either!"

Thursday — June 20

A good man will not hesitate to admit that he is in the wrong. He takes comfort in knowing he is wiser today than he was yesterday.

Friday — June 21

And what is so rare as a day in June?
Then, if ever, come perfect days;
The Heaven tries earth if it be in tune,
And over it softly her warm ear lays;
Whether we look, or whether we listen,
We hear life murmur, or see it glisten;
Every clod feels a stir of might,
An instinct within it that reaches and towers,
And, groping blindly above it for lights
Climbs to a soul in grass and flower.

— *James Russell Lowell*

Saturday — June 22

What better way to celebrate summer's arrival than with a picnic.

This morning Marg made up a truly delectable basket of food and the group of us set off for a country drive and old-fashioned picnic.

Marg, Bruce, Phyllis, Bill, Marshall and his new friend Jamie Ann, and I spent a most enjoyable time driving down the peninsula toward Niagara-on-the-Lake.

We stopped at a lovely park near Niagara and enjoyed Marg's lunch. She really outdid herself today! Cold chicken, croissants, fresh fruit cocktail, homemade lemonade all tasted so delicious in the fresh outdoor air by the lake.

I couldn't think of any better way to enjoy our first summer Saturday.

SUNDAY — JUNE 23

NOT everyone that saith unto me, "Lord, Lord," shall enter into the Kingdom of Heaven, but he that doeth the will of my Father which is in heaven.

— *Matthew 7:21*

MONDAY — JUNE 24

THE story of love is not important — what is important is that one is capable of love. It is perhaps the only glimpse we are permitted of eternity.

— *Helen Hayes*

TUESDAY — JUNE 25

HAPPINESS is possible only when one is busy. The body must toil, the mind must be occupied, and the heart must be satisfied. Those who do good, as opportunity offers, are sowing seed all the time, and they need not doubt the harvest.

WEDNESDAY — JUNE 26

ONE of the annoying things about weather forecasts is that they are not wrong all the time, either.

THURSDAY — JUNE 27

I am so busy these days planning for my upcoming trip to England. It is a full month before I leave but I do so enjoy thinking about all that Peggy and I will be doing.

Jake Frampton has been a wonderful help to me. Each day he brings more travel brochures or books on England for me to read. Although this is not my first trip abroad there are many places of interest that I have not been able to see on previous trips.

Jake has travelled to the English countryside on many occasions and he is making lists for me of things that he feels Peggy and I will enjoy seeing.

Peggy, of course, is English and very familiar with the tiny villages that abound in the Cotswolds.

I am trying to restrict my baggage to just one suitcase. I must however include at least one hat (in case Her Majesty should want me to pop over for tea). I am being silly, but in England hats are worn many more places than here in Canada.

Each day I get more excited about my upcoming trip. I can think of few things that have given me more pleasure than the anticipation of this visit to Peggy's home.

FRIDAY — JUNE 28

THE family, like the home in which they live, needs to be kept in repair, lest some little rift in the walls should appear and let in the wind and the rain. The happiness of a family depends very much on attention to little things. Order, comfort, regularity, cheerfulness, good taste, pleasant conversation — these are the ornaments of daily life, deprived of which it degenerates into a wearisome routine. There must be light in the dwelling, and brightness and pure spirits and cheerful smiles.

— *Benjamin Jowett*

SATURDAY — JUNE 29

WHAT counts is not the number of hours you put in, but how much you put in the hours.

SUNDAY — JUNE 30

SIX days shall work be done, but on the seventh day there shall be to you an holy day, a sabbath of rest to the Lord."

— *Exodus 35:2*

July

Monday — July 1

Today is our national day, Canada Day.

When the Fathers of Confederation were preparing the foundations for our country, one of the problems they faced was deciding on a name for the new country. Some of the suggestions were Laurentia, Ursalia, Mesopelagia, Albionora, Borealia, Colonia, Hochelaga, Efisga, Tuponia, and Canada.

"Canada" is the answer given by the Iroquois to the explorer Jacques Cartier's question about what they called their land. It is now believed that the word means "a collection of huts," and that the Indians had thought he was asking about their nearby village.

I'm glad that the Fathers chose Canada. I can't imagine wishing anyone a Happy Mesopelagia Day!

TUESDAY — JULY 2

OUR garden is coming along so beautifully, thanks to Will's help.

Our geraniums are blooming just perfectly and the petunias are adding to the magnificent colours.

Will stopped by to see our handiwork and he was impressed with the overall look of the yard this year.

He also had a story to tell us about a friend, John, and his garden.

John went with Will to the greenhouse yesterday to search for eight-inch-high red geraniums.

"I'm sorry but our stock is sold right out. We do have some very lovely red begonias."

"Well no, not this time," John said with resignation. "You see my wife is coming home tomorrow and it was a planter full of geraniums that I was supposed to water while she was away."

WEDNESDAY — JULY 3

IT is in loving, not in being loved, that the heart is blessed. It is in giving, not in seeking gifts, that we find our quest. Whatever be your longing or your need, that give. So shall your soul be fed, and you, indeed, shall live.

Thursday — July 4

The fourth of July is the most important American celebration of the year. The "Glorious Fourth" is celebrated with tremendous enthusiasm by all Americans.

Canadians often see Americans as brash, self-confident, blunt, independent, fearless, and impatient — but we could choose no better people in the world to have as neighbours. On this day, all Canadians join together in wishing our southern friends a happy birthday.

Friday — July 5

First, April, she with mellow showers
Opens the way for early flowers;
Then after her comes smiling May,
In a more rich and sweet array;
Next enters June, and brings us more
Gems than those two, that went before:
Then, lastly, July comes, and she
More wealth brings in than all those three.

— *Robert Herrick*

Saturday — July 6

Throughout life, our worst weaknesses and meannesses are usually committed for the sake of the people whom we most despise.

— *Charles Dickens*

Sunday — July 7

Train up a child in the way that he should go and when he is old he will not depart from it.

— *Proverbs 22:6*

Monday — July 8

Just north of the city of Toronto is the charming little village of Kleinburg. A beautiful and picturesque place, it is well worth a visit for an afternoon, or longer if you have the time!

There are a number of interesting stops to make. Perhaps the best known of the shops in Kleinburg is the "Mouse House." The tiny picket fence and miniature mail box lead to the mousehole-shaped door that opens to a fantasy shopping experience for both young and old.

The Doctor's House and Livery is a very popular place for lunch, afternoon tea, or dinner. It is a beautifully restored country doctor's home and the food is superb.

There are many small shops and galleries to be seen and no trip to Kleinburg would be complete without a visit to the McMichael Gallery, home of many of the famous Group of Seven paintings. Kleinburg is a delightful place to visit.

TUESDAY — JULY 9

THIS is Phyllis and Bill's second anniversary and I can think of no better gift than the one they received this morning.

Just before nine this morning Phyllis delivered two beautiful, small, healthy babies. Our joy knows no bounds! The doctor assured us that even though they are quite tiny, they are both perfect and in excellent condition.

Phyllis is tired, of course, but she sounded wonderful on the telephone when she called.

Jenny weighed just three pounds and Justin was larger at three pounds twelve ounces.

"What could be more perfect Gram? A boy and a girl on our first try."

Bill was scarcely coherent. When he tried to call his parents with the joyous news he forgot their phone number and had to rush back to get it from Phyllis.

Bill has delivered many babies in his own practice but, as he found out, there is nothing to compare with personal experience. Bill stayed with Phyllis all through labour and delivery and an old classmate of his delivered both babies.

The babies may be staying in the hospital for a few weeks until they weigh five pounds, but this certainly doesn't bother their parents. We praise the Lord for his many blessings.

Wednesday — July 10

My first glimpse of the twins left me awe-struck! When the nurse brought the two tiny bassinettes to the window for us to see them, I could scarcely believe my eyes.

Jenny was sleeping in a curled up position and she looked so very tiny it was hard to believe that she was real. Justin was howling and waving both arms and legs. I wonder if this is an indication of things to come?

They are both beautiful babies and Phyllis and Bill are justifiably proud parents.

Thursday — July 11

Summer days are so relaxing. The hazy warmth just makes me feel like sitting in the shade of a tree and reading.

Luckily for me, my neighbour Mrs. McGuiness often has this same inclination and we two head for the shade of her willow tree with lawn chairs and a large pitcher of icy cold lemonade.

There is something so comfortable about the companionable silence of reading with a friend. We often go for hours without speaking, but on the occasions that we feel like chatting we have someone with whom we can share our thoughts.

Friday — July 12

Last summer Canada was honoured by the visit of "Tall Ships" from around the world to our eastern provinces. I was lucky enough to see several of these majestic ships when I was on holiday last summer.

I wonder how many of us realize the importance of the role that these ships played in the development of our country.

Years before there were roads or railways, these ships were our means of trade and transportation within our own country, as well as with other countries of the world.

Without these magnificent sailing vessels our trade would have been virtually impossible.

They provided our means of transport and brought about our original trades with European countries.

To see these ships, sails set, was an unforgettable experience. It was difficult to imagine that only one hundred short years ago these ships abounded in the Great Lakes and the St. Lawrence River.

It is truly remarkable that so many people around the world are interested enough in these beautiful crafts that a whole fleet of Tall Ships is maintained for our viewing pleasure.

SATURDAY — JULY 13

ONLY two weeks away from my trip to England. I can scarcely control my excitement.

Peggy is going to meet me at Heathrow airport and we plan to stay several days in London. It has been many years since I was last in this great city and I am most anxious to see how it has changed in my absence.

One thing is certain. The people will not have changed at all.

SUNDAY — JULY 14

WAIT on the Lord: Be of good courage, and he shall strengthen thine heart: Wait, I say, on the Lord.

— *Psalm 27:14*

MONDAY — JULY 15

I never knew a night so black
Light failed to follow on its track.
I never knew a storm so gray,
It failed to have its clearing day.
I never knew such bleak despair,
That there was not a rift, somewhere,
I never knew an hour so drear,
Love could not fill it full of cheer.

Tuesday — July 16

Phyllis has come home from the hospital today, and although it was a little disappointing to leave without the babies she told me that it could be a blessing in disguise.

She will now have a little time to get her strength back and to get everything organized for their homecoming.

When the babies come home Marg is going to stay with Phyllis to help her become used to being a mother.

Both Phyllis and Bill are thrilled that Marg is able to give them her assistance.

"After all," said Bill, "look what a great job she did with Phyllis!"

Wednesday — July 17

As torrents in summer, half dried in their channels,
Suddenly rise, 'tho the sky is still cloudless,
For rain has been falling far off at their fountains;
So hearts that are fainting grow full to o'erflowing,
And they that behold it marvel, and know not
That God at their fountains,
so far off has been raining.

Thursday — July 18

I received a wonderful letter from my great-grandson Mickey today.

Mickey is having his first experience away from home. He is attending a summer camp in northern Ontario and, judging from his letter, is enjoying it immensely.

I feel that summer camp can be a wonderful experience for a child. It is very important to be sure, however, that a child is ready for this step. Some children at age seven could go away to camp and have a terrific time, while others aren't ready for it until the age of fifteen.

How well I remember my grandson Fred and his camp experience. He was very keen to go away to camp but he changed his mind after he got there. For his own reasons, he wanted to come home. At first the camp director suggested that his parents not call or visit, but Fred managed to sneak away and call home. He was nearly hysterical. "If you love me, come and get me!" His parents gave in. Two years later, he returned to the same camp and loved every minute of it.

Mickey is perfectly content this time and is already writing about "next year." I am glad, for his sake.

Friday — July 19

Jake has become quite a baseball fan. Since Toronto received a major league franchise Jake has been one of the Blue Jays' staunchest fans. Several years ago he purchased season tickets and he and his friend John attend nearly every home game.

Although I also enjoy baseball, and other sports, I confess that I find the salaries that athletes receive to be mind boggling.

What of the struggling young doctor who spends years of his time in study and then the rest of his life serving humanity? Does the doctor not deserve to be paid more than the athlete? What of the many people who work hard, with little recognition and for little money, in jobs that are essential to the smooth running of our society — farmers, bus drivers, secretaries, and, of course, mothers?

I feel the same way about movie and television personalities. Why do they receive such exorbitant amounts of money for doing so little?

I am not belittling the contribution that athletes or film stars make to society. We need these people in our lives.

I do see the amount that these people are paid as an injustice, however. I feel sure that I am not the first to feel this way.

SATURDAY — JULY 20

THERE'S only one corner of the universe you can be certain of improving, and that's your own self. So you have to begin there, not outside, not on other people. That comes afterwards, when you have worked on your own corner.

— *Aldous Huxley*

SUNDAY — JULY 21

EXCEPT ye be converted, and become as little children, ye shall not enter the Kingdom of Heaven.

Whosoever therefore shall humble himself as a little child, the same is the greatest in the Kingdom of Heaven.

— *Matthew 18:3–4*

MONDAY — JULY 22

EACH new day is an opportunity to start all over again — to cleanse our minds and hearts anew and to clarify our vision. And let us not clutter up today with the leavings of other days.

Tuesday — July 23

In those vernal seasons of the year, when the air is calm and pleasant, it were an injury and sullenness against Nature not to go out, and see her riches, and partake in her rejoicing with heaven and earth.

— *John Milton*

Wednesday — July 24

Today is the birthdate of the famous American pilot, Amelia Earhart.

Miss Earhart was a true pioneer spirit. She was trained as a nurse but she wanted to learn to fly. And fly she did!

After her training in California she moved to Boston where she kept up her aviation interests.

Her two greatest achievements were her solo crossing of the Atlantic in May of 1932 and her solo Pacific flight from Hawaii to California in January 1935.

She lost her life in an attempted flight around the world but, thanks to her daring enterprise, the field of aviation opened to women.

THURSDAY — JULY 25

WORRY never climbed a hill,
Worry never paid a bill,
Worry never dried a tear,
Worry never calmed a fear,
Worry never darned a heel,
Worry never cooked a meal,
Worry helps us not one bit,
So with you let it never sit.

FRIDAY — JULY 26

PLANTING, growing, and gardening, can sometimes be difficult for the impatient person.

Children in particular find the wait for plants to grow almost intolerable. Young Donald and John, our neighbours, decided that they wanted a garden of their own to grow vegetables. Although it is very late in the season to start a garden their father cheerfully helped dig a large area of sod out of the yard. They then churned the soil, added fertilizer, and raked the bed smooth. The seeds were planted Tuesday evening and this morning the boys came over nearly in tears.

"Mrs. McCann, we worked so hard! We planted those seeds on Tuesday and that is the last we've seen of them."

Saturday — July 27

ALTHOUGH it is very late, I can't seem to sleep yet, so I am writing in the dim lights of the airplane's cabin.

I find it so difficult to imagine that just a few hours from now I will land in England, more than three thousand miles from home.

It was quite late when we boarded the plane in Toronto but, even so, the attendants served a truly delightful dinner. I really appreciated my meal because I hadn't been able to eat much today — my excitement was too great.

We had a perfectly prepared steak, potatoes, carrots, salad, and dessert. The tea was a delicious English blend, a warm up for our arrival, I suppose.

After dinner the stewardesses handed us blankets and pillows and I did try to go to sleep but to no avail.

My seat mate is awake and reading. She is returning to England to see a daughter and grandchildren, several of whom she has never met. Her excitement level matches my own.

As we head out over the ocean, I can imagine what sailors setting sail on ships must have felt. "The Lord guides the ship."

Sunday — July 28

THE kingdom of heaven is like unto treasure hid in a field; the which when a man hath found, he hideth, and for joy thereof goeth and selleth all that he hath, and buyeth that field.

— *Matthew 13:44*

Monday — July 29

PEGGY looks marvellous! I saw her immediately at the airport and it was as if time had stood still since I last saw her.

Her beautiful English complexion is unchanged, her blue eyes still sparkle, and her white hair suits her perfectly.

We must have sounded like two schoolgirls as the two of us chattered non-stop.

Peggy had thrown caution to the wind and hired a cab to take us to our hotel in London.

It was charming to hear "Oill get them bags, m'um" from our driver as he escorted us to his limousine-like taxi.

It was strange to be driving on the "wrong" side of the road but since Peggy and I were talking at such a great rate I scarcely noticed.

Tonight is early to bed to catch up to the time change and then it's off to sightsee tomorrow.

Tuesday — July 30

I am totally charmed with our hotel! Peggy found this marvellous place many years ago and has stayed here regularly ever since.

The Basil Street is a thoroughly British hotel. Located in Knightsbridge, just a few steps from Harrods, it is the epitome of British hospitality.

No rooms are alike, each being decorated with different types of furniture. My room has two high beds, a lovely Queen Ann desk and a gigantic armoire. The maid comes in the evening to take off the spread and turn down the blankets.

If I wish to have my "boots blacked," I simply leave my shoes outside my door at night and they are returned by morning.

Peggy and I had tea at the Parrot Club, (for ladies only) and the smoked salmon sandwiches were superb.

This is not a large hotel, but the staff is gracious and Peggy and I have been made to feel most welcome.

My system still has some catching up to do so we plan just a short walk to Harrods Department Store and an early dinner before bed.

Wednesday — July 31

The world is moved not only by the mighty shoves of the heroes, but also by the aggregate of the tiny pushes of each honest worker.

August

Thursday — August 1

BOTH in England and in North America, the month of August is one of the most beautiful of the year. The flowers are at their loveliest, the crops are coming along toward harvest, and the weather seems to be perfect. This poem by Celia Thaxter entitled "August" says it well.

Buttercup nodded and said good-bye
Clover and daisy went off together,
But the fragrant water lilies lie
Yet moored in the golden August weather.

The swallows chatter about their flight,
The cricket chirps like a rare good fellow,
The asters twinkle in clusters bright
While the corn grows ripe and the apples
  mellow.

FRIDAY — AUGUST 2

PEGGY and I had a delightful time in London.

We found that the easiest way to see London was to take the double-decker sightseeing bus tour that left from Picadilly Circus. Our bus driver had a very pleasant voice and he knew the city so well that I feel as if we saw all of it in two short hours.

Buckingham Palace, Westminster Abbey, Big Ben were just as impressive as ever.

In the late afternoon we attended the Evensong service at Westminster Abbey. It was sung by the young boys choir and, as we sang by candlelight in this enormous old church, I couldn't help but wish George could have been there to hear it.

After a very late tea we rounded out our tour by attending the theatre. What trip to London would be complete without seeing Agatha Christie's *The Mousetrap* at St. Martin's Theatre? This show, unbelievably, is in its 33rd year!

Back at the hotel, we retired to the lounge where the night porter served us a delightful late evening tea complete with sandwiches and small cakes for dessert.

Tomorrow we head for the Cotswolds.

SATURDAY — AUGUST 3

MONEY and time are the heaviest burdens of life, and the unhappiest of all mortals are those who have more of either than they know how to use.

SUNDAY — AUGUST 4

LOVE divine, all loves excelling,
Joy of heaven, to earth come down,
Fix in us thy humble dwelling,
All thy faithful mercies crown.
Jesus thou art all compassion
Pure unbounded love thou art,
Visit us with thy salvation,
Enter every trembling heart.

— *Hymn 241, Charles Wesley*

MONDAY — AUGUST 5

WE believe we can change things according to our wishes because that's the only happy solution we can see. We don't think of what usually happens and what is also a happy solution: things don't change, but by and by our wishes change.

— *Marcel Proust*

Tuesday — August 6

I hope that some time every one of my readers has the opportunity to see the Cotswold area in England.

Mere words are a poor medium with which to describe the beauty of this part of England. The homes are made from a limestone that is quite golden in texture. They have prominent gables, a low steeply pitched tiled roof or a thatched straw roof, casement windows with stone mullions and transoms.

Each home usually has beautiful climbing roses on the outside walls and many have the vines climbing right to the thatched straw roof.

The towns are scattered over the rolling countryside and joined by narrow roads banked with hedges.

Freestone walls line the fields where the sheep graze. It is difficult to remember that these walls and homes have stood here for centuries with few if any changes.

Our first stop was in Burford, one of the Cotswolds' finest market towns. We ate lunch in a small tea house halfway down the Main Street hill. There was a tiny stone, marked with the date 1592, on the front wall of the building and I couldn't help but wonder at the workmanship that allows buildings to stand for 400 years without blemish.

Wednesday — August 7

PEGGY and I spent some time browsing in stores in Stow-on-the-Wold, another of the many towns in the area.

There are many lovely shops and I was attracted to a toy store with antique dolls in its window.

Inside there was a very distinguished looking gentleman watching an electric model train. This train stopped at stations, whistled, and blew smoke.

"I say," said the gentleman, "would you be so good as to wrap that for me?"

"Certainly sir, I'm sure that your grandson will love it."

"Why you're absolutely right young man. I'll take two."

Peggy and I could scarcely smother our smiles.

Thursday — August 8

SO long as enthusiasm lasts, so long is youth still with us.

Friday — August 9

WORRY is interest paid on trouble before it is due.

SATURDAY — AUGUST 10

PEGGY and I spent today exploring an ancient castle. Sudeley Castle's history is long and fascinating. In the course of a thousand years the property has changed hands more than a dozen times, has more than once been a royal residence, and has played host to at least six kings and queens.

The Lady Elizabeth Ashcombe and her husband own and maintain Sudeley for the viewing pleasure of many thousands of visitors each year.

The castle apartments have been renovated and many rooms are now open to view for the first time. A series of rooms in the old dungeon tower and the southwest wing contain what is possibly the largest collection of toys and playthings from the past that is in existence.

Sudeley Castle has magnificent gardens, which were laid out during the restoration of the castle in the nineteenth century.

Later in the afternoon we were also entertained by a wonderful display of falconry in the garden area.

As usual the nicest part of our visit was meeting the many other castle visitors and enjoying conversations with them.

SUNDAY — AUGUST 11

O How lovely are thy tabernacles, O Lord of hosts!
My soul longeth, yea, even fainteth for the courts of the Lord:
My heart and my flesh crieth out for the living God.

— *Psalm 84:1–2*

MONDAY — AUGUST 12

I wonder if Alexander Graham Bell had any inkling of the effect that his invention would have on our world.

Yesterday I talked with Marg on the telephone. Marg was some three thousand miles away, across an ocean, and yet her voice was as loud and clear as if she were in a room beside me.

She had wonderful news from home. Phyllis and Bill's twins, Justin and Jenny, are coming home today.

In a little more than a month they have put on enough weight to allow them to leave the hospital safely.

Everyone is very excited, of course, and I look forward to seeing them all next week.

I love to travel but it is nice to have the telephone as that special link to home.

TUESDAY — AUGUST 13

ONE of the most pleasurable parts of this trip to England has been the company of the many people that we have met.

We lunched several days at a delightful little inn in the tiny village of Stanton, and by the end of our second meal had met the owners and the people who were fellow patrons.

In Canada it is a rare occasion when another person dining speaks with you. Here in England it is accepted as warm hospitality to speak to your neighbouring lunch partners.

"Truly fine weather, isn't it?"

"Don't miss seeing the vicar's garden. It's simply smashing."

People seem very outgoing and friendly and yet they wouldn't think of invading your privacy by asking personal questions. If you wish to volunteer any information they are wonderful listeners and very interested in your stories of "Canader."

One very lovely lady, who was lunching alone, asked if Peggy and I would like to see a "Cotswold" home. She then invited us to her home in the village for tea that afternoon. We were given a grand tour and a very lovely tea. I'm sure this happens only in England.

WEDNESDAY — AUGUST 14

FAR better it is to dare mighty things, to win glorious triumphs, even though checkered by failure, than to take rank with those poor spirits who neither enjoy much nor suffer much, because they live in the gray twilight that knows not victory nor defeat.

— *Theodore Roosevelt*

THURSDAY — AUGUST 15

WILLIAM Blake's poem "Night" is one of my favourites.

The sun descending in the west,
The evening star does shine;
The birds are silent in their nest,
And I must seek for mine.
The moon, like a flower,
In heaven's high bower,
With silent delight
Sits and smiles on the night.

Farewell, green fields and happy groves,
Where flocks have took delight,
Where lambs have nibbled, silent moves
The feet of angels bright;
Unseen they pour blessing,
And joy without ceasing,
On each bud and blossom,
And each sleeping bosom.

Friday — August 16

I can scarcely believe that my visit to England is nearly ended. Peggy and I met so many new friends, saw so many new places, and saw so many interesting things that the time has flown by.

I will have an array of memories to look back on for years to come.

Saturday — August 17

A man would do well to carry a pencil in his pocket and write down the thoughts of the moment. Those that come unsought are commonly the most valuable and should be secured because they seldom return.

— *Francis Bacon*

Sunday — August 18

When I consider thy heavens, the work of thy fingers, and the moon and the stars, which thou hast ordained;

What is man, that thou art mindful of him? And the son of man, that thou visitest him?

— *Psalm 8:3–4*

Monday — August 19

A man who acts on impulse may sometimes be laughed at for his mistakes, but he will frequently attain to higher things, and be much better loved by his fellows than the colder, more calculating logician who rarely makes a blunder.

— *Farnol*

Tuesday — August 20

After a wonderful vacation I am really happy to be home. There is almost nothing that can take the place of your own bed at night, your own china tea cup, and a stroll around your own garden in the evening.

Other places may be more beautiful, have greener grass, more coloured flowers — but none can replace the home or room of your own. The heart carries a special place for these.

Wednesday — August 21

When Phyllis brought the twins over today I couldn't take my eyes from wee Justin's face. The resemblance that he bears to George is truly amazing. I suppose I sound like a true great-grandmother now, don't I?

Thursday — August 22

The Christian Golden Rule is an unwritten law the world over. It bears a varied interpretation, but the principle has never been compromised. Here are a few variations.

Do as you would be done by.

— *Persian*

Do not do that to a neighbour which you would take ill from him.

— *Greek*

One should seek for others the happiness one desires for oneself.

— *Buddhist*

What you would not wish done to yourself, do not do unto others.

— *Chinese*

The rule of life is to guard and do by the things of others as they do by their own.

— *Hindu*

Let none of you treat his brother in a way he himself would dislike to be treated.

— *Muslim*

FRIDAY — AUGUST 23

RESILIENCY is an important factor in living. The winds of life may bend us, but if we have resilience of spirit, they cannot break us.

To courageously straighten again after our heads have been bowed by defeat, disappointment, and suffering is the supreme test of character.

SATURDAY — AUGUST 24

THE most agreeable of all companions is a simple, frank man, without any high pretensions to oppressive greatness.

— *Lessing*

SUNDAY — AUGUST 25

FOR one day in thy courts is better than a thousand.
I had rather be a doorkeeper in the house of my God than to dwell in the tents of ungodliness.
For the Lord God is a sun and shield; the Lord shall give grace and glory: and no good thing shall be withheld from them that lead a godly life.

O Lord God of hosts, blessed is the man that putteth his trust in thee.

— *Psalm 84*

Monday — August 26

Jake stopped by this evening to hear all about my trip to England. We had a most enjoyable time discussing castles, gardens, book stores, and whatnots. Jake has been abroad several times and was very familiar with many of the sights that Peggy and I took in together.

Jake's great love in England is the wide variety of bookstores to be found in every city, town, or village. Many of the stores deal uniquely in antique books and Jake has been fortunate enough to find many interesting and very rare old books.

Although Jake has a bookstore, many of the books that he has collected belong to his personal collection and are not available to his customers.

In a small bookstore in the town of Broadway, I was lucky enough to find a rare edition of Dickens's *David Copperfield*. I brought it home for Jake and I don't think a block of gold could have pleased him more.

I was overjoyed to see his pleasure. Nothing is more gratifying than giving a gift that is so enthusiastically received.

Tuesday — August 27

All people smile in the same language.

WEDNESDAY — AUGUST 28

MY, how the warm summer days fly by. The nights are cooling now, perhaps to give us a hint of fall weather to come.

Mary McConnell walked over for tea with several of her children today.

"So many people say to me 'I'll bet you can hardly wait for school to start' that I just give a nod now, instead of trying to explain to them that I wish the summer would never end. The summer is the one time during a year that our whole family can be together regularly. We all work our garden together, and the children take real pride in being able to help out their older brothers and sisters with the chores.

"It is so nice for all of us to go on a picnic and really have the time to listen to each other's ideas and discuss our opinions on all kinds of topics.

"When the children go back to school the schedule becomes full so quickly. There are sports, music lessons, homework, and a variety of other things that mean we can rarely all see each other at one time.

"Forgive me if I feel selfish and wish summer would never end, Edna, but it is the truth."

Thursday — August 29

How stubbornly I cleared the field
And pulverized the stony land
And watered all its sterile sand
To make the barren acres yield.

But when I gained the victory
And moulded to my will the ground,
I rested from my work and found
The subtle earth had moulded me.

— *Lewis Morgan*

Friday — August 30

The highest reward for a man's toil is not what he gets for it, but rather what he becomes by it.

Saturday — August 31

"You have a marvellous gift for oratory," said a reporter to George Bernard Shaw. "How did you develop it?"

Shaw replied, "I learned to speak as men learn to skate or cycle, by doggedly making a fool of myself until I got used to it."

September

Sunday — September 1

When visiting some old friends in Vermont, U.S.A., we attended a local church.

Leafing through their new Book of Common Prayer before the service began, I discovered a beautiful prayer for seniors like myself.

Look with mercy, O God our Father, on those whose increasing years bring them weakness, distress, or isolation. Provide for them homes of dignity and peace; give them understanding helpers and the willingness to accept help; and as their strength diminishes, increase their faith and their awareness of your love. Amen.

MONDAY — SEPTEMBER 2

Labour Day

LABOUR Day was a very important day for George. He had great sympathy for working men and women, born out of his own experiences in the Great Depression. He knew about men finding food and friends at the soup kitchen, and beds in the church basement. He saw and felt the hurt of the thousands of unemployed and I think the experience of trying to help these men made him the sensitive and caring person that he was.

Now some fifty years later, after a period of economic growth and affluence, many hundred thousands are facing the same hurt of unemployment and its related problems.

I find it strange that we can put a man on the moon but cannot provide enough jobs for honest workers.

I hope that our next Labour Day will see many more of our unemployed back in the work force and our country once again using "the only true freedom — the freedom to work."

TUESDAY — SEPTEMBER 3

IF you don't scale the mountain, you can't see the view.

Wednesday — September 4

The children have returned to school and I miss the noisy chatter during the day.

It's amazing how quiet our neighbourhood is without the happy shouts of laughter that go with summer vacation.

For all of their grumbling most of the children are secretly delighted to get back into the classroom. Many of their friends have returned from summer camp or cottages and the next few weeks will hear never-ending stories of all the fun times the children enjoyed.

Thursday — September 5

Here's a health to the future,
A sigh for the past;
We can love and remember,
And hope to the last;
And, for all the base lies
That the almanacs hold,
While there's love in the heart,
We can never grow old.

Friday — September 6

All one's life is music, if one touched the notes rightly and in tune.

— *Ruskin*

SATURDAY — SEPTEMBER 7

SOME people have a rare gift and are unaware of possessing it. The ability to treat sick people as if they were truly themselves, is to my mind, a remarkable talent.

I like to tell about Jack Jones, an old friend, who is one who possesses this gift.

Several years ago a very dear friend of Jack's and mine had a brain tumor. Although Neal's mind was alert his power of speech was badly affected. His physical appearance, as well, changed dramatically. The loss of weight and the loss of his hair altered his appearance, but the twinkle in his eye remained, and a smile was not far from his lips.

Many of Neal's friends did not know how to handle his illness. Some simply didn't visit at all, while others who did were so uncomfortable that the conversations and visits were brief and unproductive.

Jack Jones was the shining exception. He would drop in regularly, as usual, and talk about the things that they always talked about. The fact that Neal couldn't always reply or that his responses were garbled didn't bother Jack at all. "I know what you mean" was his answer to Neal and, in fact, he always did! Jack is a remarkable man.

SUNDAY — SEPTEMBER 8

IT was Rally Day at church this morning. Many parents and children returned to worship after a summer of holidays and weekends out of town. The church was alive with children. Our pastor called them all forward and welcomed them back before sending them along to the church school.

It gave me a lift to feel that we were truly a "family" of believers — children, young couples, middle-aged, and seniors — all sharing in the worship of a God of love, and sharing that love with one another. I feel truly blessed from such an experience.

MONDAY — SEPTEMBER 9

WE should always have in our heads one free and open corner where we can give place, or lodging as they pass, to the ideas of our friends. It really becomes unbearable to converse with men whose brains are divided into well-filled pigeon-holes, where nothing can enter from outside. Let us have hospitable hearts and minds.

— *Joseph Joubert*

Tuesday — September 10

Henry Van Dyke wrote this tribute to "The Unknown Teacher." I think it is marvellous.

I sing the praises of the unknown teacher.

Famous educators plan new systems of pedagogy, but it is the unknown teacher who delivers and guides the young.

He lives in obscurity and contends with hardship. He keeps the watch along the borders of darkness and makes the attack on the trenches of ignorance and folly.

Patient in his daily duty he strives to conquer the evil powers which are the enemy of youth.

He awakens sleeping spirits.

He quickens the indolent, encourages the eager, and steadies the unstable. He communicates his own joy in learning and shares with boys and girls the best treasures of his mind. He lights many candles which, in later years, will shine back to cheer him.

This is his reward.

Knowledge may be gained from books; but the love of knowledge is transmitted only by personal contact.

No one has deserved better of the republic than the unknown teacher.

Wednesday — September 11

Grow old along with me!
The best is yet to be,
The last of life, for which the first was made:
Our times are in His hand
Who saith, "A whole I planned,
Youth sows but half; trust God: see all, nor be
afraid."

— *Robert Browning*

Thursday — September 12

My son-in-law Bruce brought me this little story after dinner this evening. It points out the value of over-reacting (something for which Bruce has become quite well-known).

A fellow found himself in the middle of a pasture with an angry bull charging him. The only escape in sight was a tree, but the nearest limb was ten feet off the ground. The fellow ran and made a great leap. He missed the limb on the way up, but caught it on the way down.

Friday — September 13

Friendship is the shadow of the evening, which strengthens with the setting sun of life.

— *LaFontaine*

Saturday — September 14

My stay in London has made me very interested in that wonderful city.

London was founded in Roman times and was originally called Londonium. Because it was the focus of the Roman road system in Britain, it soon became Roman Britain's most important settlement. Although Londonium's importance diminished after the Romans left Britain, it again became England's most important town in the period before the Norman Conquest. Its position in English life has not changed since then. As England's power and wealth increased, so did London's. It became the chief port in Europe and, shortly after 1800, became the first city to exceed one million in population. It is now one of the world's great cultural capitals, containing many museums, art galleries, theatres, concert halls, and architectural treasures, as well as being the spiritual home of English-language literature. I am sure most visitors would agree with the sentiments expressed by Samuel Johnson in 1777:

"When a man is tired of London, he is tired of life; for there is in London all that life can afford."

SUNDAY — SEPTEMBER 15

AND Jesus said, "I am the Way, the Truth and the Life."

— *John 14:6*

MONDAY — SEPTEMBER 16

POETRY has been to me its own exceeding great reward; it has given me the habit of wishing to discover the good and beautiful in all that meets and surrounds me.

— *Coleridge*

TUESDAY — SEPTEMBER 17

THE football season is in full swing again and I do enjoy watching the occasional game on television.

I think you will enjoy this football story from my neighbour.

He was watching a game on television and in the heat of the play spoke to no one in particular.

"That quarterback is hopeless! He hasn't hit one receiver all day and he's fumbled twice. Why don't they take him out of the game?"

His son, with a child's logic, said, "It's probably his ball, Dad."

Wednesday — September 18

We, in our country, are fortunate to have volunteers for so many important jobs in our society.

These people help in so many ways. There are mothers who help supervise school field trips. There are the men and women who organize cancer fund-raisers. There are Big Brothers and Big Sisters who help children in single parent families. There are the candy-stripers in the hospitals who bring juice to patients when the nurse is too busy.

Without these volunteers many of us would be unable to struggle through our misfortunes alone and the cost of their services would be so prohibitive that we would be unable to utilize them even if they were available.

A Statistics Canada survey five years ago showed that 2.7 million persons worked 374 million hours of volunteer unpaid service. If these people had been receiving Canada's minimum wage the payment would have been twelve million dollars. This would have come directly from the taxpayers.

Perhaps the next time you see one of our volunteers you could give them a personal thank you for all the time that is so unselfishly given.

Thursday — September 19

LIFE would be infinitely happier if we could only be born at the age of eighty and gradually approach eighteen.

— *Mark Twain*

Friday — September 20

THERE is nothing I can give you which you have not, but there is much that while I cannot give you, you can take:

No heaven can come to us unless our hearts find rest in it today. Take heaven.

No peace lies in the future which is not hidden in this present instant. Take Peace.

The gloom of the world is but a shadow; behind it, yet within reach, is joy. Take Joy.

Saturday — September 21

AUTUMN is a beautiful time of year. The colours are so bright and gay. They bring to mind two lines from Isla Richardson:

"Autumn is a gypsy
With jewels in her hair."

SUNDAY — SEPTEMBER 22

IT is a good thing to give thanks unto the Lord, and to sing praises unto thy Name, O Thou Most High.

To tell of Thy loving kindness in the morning and of Thy faithfulness every night.

Psalm 92:1–2

MONDAY — SEPTEMBER 23

IF anyone tell thee that he has searched for knowledge and not attained it, believe him not; if he tell thee he has attained knowledge without searching for it, believe him not, but if he tell thee he has searched for knowledge and attained it, thou mayest believe him.

— The Talmud

TUESDAY — SEPTEMBER 24

A confession that you were wrong is proof that you know more than you thought you knew.

— Coleman Cox

NEIGHBOURS AID
HALL

WEDNESDAY — SEPTEMBER 25

SEPTEMBER
The goldenrod is yellow;
The corn is turning brown;
The trees in apple orchards
With fruit are bending down.

The gentians bluest fringes
Are curling in the sun;
In dusty pods the milkweed
Its hidden silk has spun

The sedges flaunt their harvest
In every meadow nook;
And asters by the brookside
Make asters in the brook.

From dewy lanes at morning
The grapes sweet odours rise;
At noon the roads all flutter
With yellow butterflies.

By all these lovely tokens
September days are here,
With summers best of weather,
And autumns best of cheer.

— *Helen Hurt Jackson*

Thursday — September 26

Farley Mowat is a Canadian author who has achieved world-wide recognition for his twenty-two books. They have been translated into over twenty languages and this is rare indeed for Canadian authors.

He was born in Belleville, Ontario in 1921, and his father, who was a librarian, was probably the spark that kindled Mowat's literary flame.

As a youngster, Mowat wrote poetry. A few years later, as his interest in nature developed, he helped form a naturalist club that published a mimeographed magazine. He took up nature photography and began to collect strange pets, including gophers, crows, and owls. Wol and Weeps, the owls, were made famous in his book *Owls in the Family* published in 1962, just as Mutt, the dog in *The Dog Who Wouldn't Be*, had become famous earlier.

Mowat, a diverse writer, has often said that he only writes about things that deeply interest him. He also is a man of strong opinions. He admires wild animals and has been heard to say that he thinks most animals are far superior to man in the way they live.

Mowat has won many literary awards including the Governor General's Literary Award. His works are well worth reading.

Friday — September 27

I have often regretted my speech, seldom my silence.

Saturday — September 28

A peck of common sense is worth a bushel of learning.

Sunday — September 29

Harvest Festival

Sing to the Lord of harvest, sing songs of love and praise.
With joyful hearts and voices your hallelujahs raise,
By Him the rolling seasons in fruitful order move,
Sing to the Lord of Harvest, a joyful song of love.
By him the clouds drop fatness, the deserts bloom and spring,
The hills leap up in gladness, the valleys laugh and sing.
He filleth with his fulness, all things with large increase,
He crowns the year with goodness, with plenty and with peace.

— *John Samuel Moncell*

Monday — September 30

Bruce and his friends are still enjoying their golf games even though the weather has cooled considerably.

This past weekend there was a duffer in their group. Time after time he would hit his brand new balls into places where they couldn't be found — into the pond, up over the railway tracks, off into the woods.

Finally one of the foursome asked why he didn't use old balls for the more difficult shots.

"An old ball?" asked the duffer. "Do I look like I have ever had an old ball?"

October

TUESDAY — OCTOBER 1

SOMETHING told the wild geese
It was time to go.
Though the fields lay golden
Something whispered, — "Snow,"
Leaves were green and stirring,
Berries luster-glossed,
But beneath warm feathers
Something cautioned, — "Frost."
All the sagging orchards
Steamed with amber spice,
But each wild breast stiffened
At remembered ice.
Something told the wild geese
It was time to fly, —
Summer sun was on their wings,
Winter in their cry.

— *Rachel Field*

Wednesday — October 2

This time of year is so very beautiful that it is almost breathtaking.

Marg and I took a drive out into the country the other day just to view the changing leaves. I don't believe that I can think of anything in this world that makes the coming of winter more acceptable than the sight of the hills aflame in the autumn sunlight. It is almost as if Nature feels obliged to imprint this magical beauty on your mind to carry you through the dreary gray days to come.

Thursday — October 3

Faith is the soul's insight or discovery of some Reality that enables a man to stand anything that can happen to him in the universe.

— *Josiah Royce*

Friday — October 4

The devil is not as black as he is painted. In fact, he is more like us than we care to admit.

Saturday — October 5

My sister Sarah still lives on the east coast of Canada. We lived, as children, on the shoreline of Nova Scotia, and although Sarah has been, for short periods of time, in other parts of the country, she always returns to the province that she knows and loves.

We have talked about this often.

"You know, Edna," Sarah will say, "You and I are very different. You enjoy yourself wherever you are, while I really only feel comfortable when I am in Nova Scotia. I get an aching in my heart and soul at the thought of spending my life elsewhere."

I know that Sarah is not alone in this feeling. Many people find one place in the world that suits them and living elsewhere simply will not do.

My brother Ben and I often used to tease Sarah about this until we realized how much her province means to her. She gets so much pleasure from knowing everyone in her small town, from seeing "her" ocean everyday, and from the sights and smells that are part of her life there, that she would, indeed, be foolish to leave Nova Scotia.

Sunday — October 6

At this time of year, most of us are very conscious of God's ancient promise to Noah and thankful for it.

And the Lord said, "While the earth remaineth, seed time and harvest, and cold and heat, and summer and winter, and day and night shall not cease."

— *Genesis 8:22*

Monday — October 7

A problem for many of us seniors is getting enough exercise to stay fit and healthy.

As time passes our physical strength diminishes and staying active seems to become more challenging.

What I have found, and my doctor, Don Gorton, agrees, is that walking is probably the easiest and safest way to keep fit.

Several short walks a day, even in poor weather, are a wonderful benefit to young and old alike.

Walking is also an excellent way to clear the mind. I seem to be able to think more clearly while walking and the fresh air usually gives me a great lift. May I heartily recommend walking to all of you.

Tuesday — October 8

Much wisdom remains to be learned, and if it is only to be learned through adversity, we must endeavour to endure adversity with what fortitude we can command. But if we can acquire wisdom soon enough, adversity may not be necessary and the future of man may be happier than any part of his past.

Wednesday — October 9

Mark Twain has always been one of my favourite authors.

This story is one that I particularly enjoy.

Mark Twain was attending a charity sermon in a church in New York. As the sermon began he took a twenty dollar bill from his pocket, ready for the collection.

As the sermon passed the fifteen minute mark he put back the twenty and substituted a ten dollar bill. As the sermon rambled on he replaced the ten in his pocket.

Eventually the sermon ended and the collection plate was passed round.

As the plate passed Twain, he put his hand in and removed a ten dollar bill.

Thursday — October 10

IT is often very tough to explain to young people that there are difficulties to face in aging.

Phyllis has a friend who teaches a family life program to high school students. He was explaining to the students that there were often hearing difficulties related to aging, as well as problems with eyesight, and so on. The students wrote their notes but the teacher felt that they couldn't really appreciate these problems without first hand knowledge.

In order for them to achieve this comprehension he devised an ingenious plan. The students were paired off for the day. In the morning one of the two students was given eyeglasses to wear that had a light coating of vaseline smeared on them. They put cotton in their ears and several pebbles in their shoes. The "seeing" partner was then to take the "aging" student somewhere in the community and to stay with them as they tried to find their way back to the school. In the afternoon their roles were reversed.

Many of the students were near to tears of frustration before they were able to return to the school. This practical demonstration gave the students a tremendous insight that no amount of lecturing could ever accomplish.

Friday — October 11

Perhaps the most valuable of all education is the ability to make yourself do the thing you have to do, when it ought to be done, whether you like it or not; it is the first lesson that ought to be learned, and however early a man's training begins, it is probably the last lesson that he learns thoroughly.

— *Thomas Huxley*

Saturday — October 12

It was on this date in 1492 that Christopher Columbus discovered America. It took a man with tenacity of purpose and unflinching devotion to a single idea, to face the perils that he faced in his attempt to reach land to the west.

"He accomplished more than anyone else towards making us masters of the world on which we tread, and giving us, instead of yawning abysses and realms of vapour, wide waters for our ships, and land for the city and the plough.... He stands in history as the completer of the globe."

— *John Sterling*

Sunday — October 13

O most merciful Father, we humbly thank Thee for all thy gifts so freely bestowed upon us — for life and health and safety, for power to work and leisure to rest, for all that is beautiful in creation and in the lives of men, but above all we thank Thee for our spiritual mercies in Christ Jesus, our Lord, who with Thee and the Holy Spirit liveth and reigneth, One Lord forever and ever. Amen.

— *Book of Common Prayer*

Monday — October 14

Thanksgiving is as late as it can be this year. We shall all have to dress warmly and wear gloves as we perform our annual Thanksgiving garden clean up.

I have always enjoyed this season but I notice the changes that have taken place over the years. In our small towns we used to burn our dried leaves, vines, and plants. The smoky smell of the bonfires was almost as sweet as that coming from the kitchen, where the goose was roasting and pumpkin pie was baking.

Now we gather all the garden waste in garbage bags and I truly miss the old odours. Even so, I am still thankful for all my blessings today.

Tuesday — October 15

I wonder how many of you know how the province of Alberta was named. I found this little bit of information in a history book and thought that you might find it interesting.

The province of Alberta was named by the Marquis of Lorne, who was Governor General from 1878–1883, for his wife H.R.H. Princess Louise Caroline Alberta. After a visit to the west he wrote:

"In token of the love which thou has shown
For this wide land of freedom, I have named
A province vast, and for its beauty famed,
By thy dear name to be hereafter known."

Wednesday — October 16

No spring, nor Summer beauty hath such grace,
As I have seen in one Autumnal face.

— *John Donne*

Thursday — October 17

Have patience with all things, but chiefly have patience with yourself. Do not lose courage in considering your own imperfections, but instantly set about remedying them — every day begin the task anew.

— *St. Francis de Sales*

Friday — October 18

A haze on the far horizon,
The infinite, tender sky,
The ripe, rich tint of the cornfields,
And the wild geese sailing high, —
And all over upland and lowland
The charm of the goldenrod, —
Some of us call it Autumn,
Some of us call it God.

— *William Herbert Carruth*

Saturday — October 19

As Mark Twain and William Dean Howells were leaving church one morning, it started to rain.

"Do you think it will stop?" asked Howells.
"It always has," answered Twain.

Sunday — October 20

Jesus said, "A new commandment give I unto you, that ye love one another; as I have loved you, that ye also love one another.

By this shall all men know that ye are my disciples, if ye have love one to another."

— *John 13:34–35*

Monday — October 21

The measure of man's real character is what he would do if he knew he would never be found out.

Tuesday — October 22

Do all the good you can
By all the means you can
In all the ways you can
In all the places you can
At all the times you can
To all the people you can
As long as ever you can

Wednesday — October 23

If we pause to think, we will have cause to thank.

THURSDAY — OCTOBER 24

THIS is a marvellous time of year for those of us who do home canning and preserving. Although it is very time consuming the end results make the hours of work seem worthwhile.

We always try to do our canning together, as it makes the job less tedious and gives us a chance for a good visit together.

This year I have decided to do preserves and baking as Christmas gifts. Many of my older friends are not able to do their own so I am going to do up Christmas hampers for them.

Phyllis, who is very artistic, is busy making decorative lid covers in red and white checkered material.

The crops have been excellent and we now have six types of fruit jellies and jams, as well as many vegetables, tomato chili, and relishes.

Perhaps those of you whose families are not close enough for a get-together could arrange a group of neighbours for a canning party. We are always delighted, in winter, that we have spent these productive few days and I'm sure you and your family would too.

FRIDAY — OCTOBER 25

A man wrapped up in himself makes a very small package.

Saturday — October 26

If we fill our hours with regrets over the failures of yesterday, and with worries over the problems of tomorrow, we have no today in which to be thankful.

Sunday — October 27

But I say unto you, love your enemies, bless them that curse you, do good to them that hate you, and pray for them which despitefully use you, and persecute you;

That ye may be the children of your Father which is in heaven: for he maketh his sun to rise on the evil and on the good, and sendeth rain on the just and on the unjust.

— *Matthew 5:44–45*

Monday — October 28

You can always spot a well informed man. His views coincide with yours.

Tuesday — October 29

Basic research is what I'm doing when I don't know what I'm doing.

— *Wernher von Braun*

Wednesday — October 30

EACH year at this time Marg comes up with new uses for our jack o'lantern leftovers.

One neighbour has a terrific idea for the seeds that are removed. She rinses them all carefully and spreads them on a cookie sheet. She adds salt and then toasts them in the oven at 350 for about ten minutes or until they are crisp. They make a terrific low calorie snack.

Marg's pumpkin cupcakes have many more calories but they are delicious. Here is her recipe.

4 tbsp. butter
4 tbsp. lard
¼ cup sugar
2 eggs
1 cup pumpkin
½ cup rich cream
2¼ cups flour
2½ tsp. baking powder
¼ tsp. baking soda
½ tsp. each of salt, cinnamon, nutmeg, and ginger.

Cream butter, lard, and sugar. Add eggs and beat. Add pumpkin and mix. Sift dry ingredients and add to first mixture. Pour into muffin tins. Bake at 350 for 25–30 minutes.

Thursday — October 31

I sat in my chair by the window this afternoon so that I could watch the parade of children in costume go off to school for Hallowe'en parties.

I am always amazed at the ingenuity that so many children and parents show at this costuming time.

Two little girls went past with enormous boxes over them painted as dice — so simple and yet so effective.

There were rabbits and bears, mice and cats, and a steady stream of robots, always a favourite with boys.

I look forward to the evening's visitors.

November

Friday — November 1

John Adams Dix wrote this poem for the month of November. I feel he has summed up this month perfectly.

No warmth, no cheerfulness, no healthful ease,
No comfortable feel in any member —
No shade, no shine, no butterflies, no bees,
No fruits, no flowers, no leaves, no birds,
November!

Saturday — November 2

Faith consists in believing when it is beyond the power of reason to believe. It is not enough that a thing be possible for it to be believed.

— *Voltaire*

SUNDAY — NOVEMBER 3

THERE is no fear in love; but perfect love casteth out fear, because fear hath torment. He that feareth is not made perfect in love. We love him, because He first loved us.

— *I John 4:18–19*

MONDAY — NOVEMBER 4

THE children in our community are frequently asking Marg or me to sponsor them in all manner of fund-raising efforts. Swim-a-thons, bike-a-thons, skate-a-thons are very popular ways to raise money for schools or charities.

One of the best "a-thons" that I know of is the read-a-thon to raise money for research in multiple sclerosis, one of the world's most terrible diseases.

Our young neighbours read as many books as they can in one month and so it is of great benefit to them as well as to the many thousands who suffer from this debilitating disease. Marg and I felt good sponsoring the boys in this worthwhile enterprise.

TUESDAY — NOVEMBER 5

WISE men are not always silent, but know when to be.

Wednesday — November 6

The really happy man is the one who can enjoy the scenery when he has to take a detour.

Thursday — November 7

Last week I visited with my grandson Fred and his family. In their den was a large wall map of the world and a globe on the side table. I commented on these and my great-grandson Mickey delighted me with his reply.

"You see, Gram," he said, "when we watch the news on T.V. with Mom and Dad the reports come from all over the world — Lebanon, Chile, Asia, or other parts of Canada and the U.S.A. One of us points out the spot on the map or the globe and it helps us to realize that we really live in a global village."

This is such an important concept to instil in their young minds. They are fortunate to have such caring parents.

Friday — November 8

It is better to sleep on what you intend doing than to stay awake over what you have done.

SATURDAY — NOVEMBER 9

ALL problems become smaller if you don't dodge them but confront them. Touch a thistle timidly and it will prick you; grasp it boldly and its spines crumble.

SUNDAY — NOVEMBER 10

O God of love, O King of peace,
Make wars throughout our world to cease,
The wrath of sinful man restrain,
Give peace O God, give peace again.

— *Henry William Baker*

MONDAY — NOVEMBER 11

Remembrance Day

ON this Remembrance Day we remember the thousands of men and women who gave their lives so that we may live in freedom and peace. Let us pray that none of our future generations will be called upon to make this great sacrifice. Let us pray for peace and harmony for all nations and that we shall indeed see "peace in our time."

Tuesday — November 12

When I was younger I dreaded the deadlines that seemed to dominate our lives. George had his weekly deadline — a new sermon to produce for each Sunday. We also had regular church activities, and community and family responsibilities each with separate deadlines forced upon us.

Wednesday — November 13

You can pitch a no hit game,
But it's just another loss
If the errors of your teammates
Put opponent's runs across.
You might be a brilliant runner
Pass and kick with easy grace,
But you'll miss the winning touchdown
If a teammate's out of place.
In the sporting world or business,
In the office or a mill,
Nothing can produce a winner
Like a little teamwork will.

Thursday — November 14

Success is picking yourself up one more time than you fall down.

FRIDAY — NOVEMBER 15

To be born a gentleman is an accident. To die one is an achievement.

SATURDAY — NOVEMBER 16

THE hockey season is back in full swing again and Jake dropped over to watch this evening's game with me. Jake has always been impressed with Wayne Gretzky's talent. He is probably the most astonishing player that the game of hockey has ever seen.

Gretzky was fortunate enough to be born with a tremendous talent and, perhaps, he also has had more than his share of good luck. But I think this little story of Jake's points out exactly what has made Wayne Gretzky so great.

One night, a couple of seasons ago, Gretzky's team, the Edmonton Oilers, played the Detroit Red Wings. Gretzky got two goals and three assists but, uncharacteristically, he missed on two breakaways. After the game his comment was, "I can't wait to get downstairs and shoot some tennis balls. I should never have missed those breakaways."

He had scored five points but felt that he could improve. This is what champions are made of!

SUNDAY — NOVEMBER 17

AND now abideth faith, hope, charity, these three; but the greatest of these is charity.

— *I Corinthians 13:13*

MONDAY — NOVEMBER 18

ALTHOUGH I am usually able to handle most things with good humour there are times when I am not able to deal with things in my usual way.

What has me down is a 'flu and cold. It always seems to happen at this time of year and I am presently wondering just how long a person can live when they are unable to breathe through the nose.

For several days now I have felt quite poorly and spent my time in bed blowing my nose and drinking orange juice and chicken soup.

Finally, today, Marg has a roaring fire going and I am going to take my Christmas cards and mailing list to sit and work by the fireplace.

I am quite sure that this task will brighten my outlook considerably.

TUESDAY — NOVEMBER 19

IF God did not exist it would be necessary to invent him.

— *Voltaire*

Wednesday — November 20

If you don't have time to do it right, when will you have time to do it over?

Thursday — November 21

At the coffee hour after church last Sunday, a group of young people were caught up in a very serious discussion about war and peace.

I came home feeling a great hope for the future.

Friday — November 22

Life is a voyage in which we choose neither vessel nor weather, but much can be done in the management of the sails and the guidance of the helm.

Saturday — November 23

I believe that any man's life will be filled with constant and unexpected encouragement if he makes up his mind to do his level best each day, and as nearly as possible reaches the high water mark of pure and useful living.

— *Booker T. Washington*

Sunday — November 24

We know that all things work together for good to them that love God, to them who are called according to his purpose.

— *Romans 8:28*

Monday — November 25

Mary and John have returned home after spending the last few months in Canada's far north. Both have hailed this trip as one of their most interesting experiences ever.

Their time was spent in and around Yellowknife, on the north shore of Great Slave Lake. Mary was fascinated with the artwork of the Inuit and she has brought back paintings and carvings of great beauty.

John found his time spent with the people in the north to be an invaluable asset to his understanding of his fellow Canadians.

I know that we will hear many stories in the days to come and I am very happy to have them back home with us.

Tuesday — November 26

Tact is the knack of making a point without making an enemy.

Wednesday — November 27

A six year old boy came home from school one day with a note from his teacher suggesting that he was "too stupid to learn" and that he be removed from school. The boy's name was Thomas A. Edison.

Thursday — November 28

Today is our American neighbours' celebration of Thanksgiving Day. Robert Louis Stevenson wrote a very beautiful "thank you" for this day.

Lord, behold our family here assembled. We thank Thee for this place in which we dwell; for the love that unites; for the peace accorded us this day; for the hope with which we expect the morrow, for the health, the work, the food, and the bright skies, that make our lives delightful; for our friends in all parts of the earth, and our friendly helpers. Let peace abound in our small company.

Friday — November 29

Marg and Bruce attended a local art show and I had to chuckle at Bruce's comments. "You know, Edna, trying to understand modern art is like trying to follow the plot in a bowl of alphabet soup."

SATURDAY — NOVEMBER 30

St. Andrew's Day

ST. Andrew, the patron saint of Scotland, was one of the most interesting of all of the twelve apostles.

Whenever he appears in the gospel stories, he is bringing someone else to Jesus — his brother Peter, a little boy with five barley loaves and a few fish, or a Greek seeking the Lord.

After bringing them to Jesus he fades into the background.

It is my experience that many devout Christians follow the example of St. Andrew and are always ready to lead others to Jesus while staying in the background themselves.

December

SUNDAY — DECEMBER 1

I enjoy this Sunday very much. It is the beginning of Advent, a season of joyful anticipation.

At the morning service the large wreath over the font will be dedicated. As the congregation says the advent collect, a child will light the first purple advent candle. The scripture lessons will tell of the prophets proclaiming the coming of the Messiah.

This is truly the beginning of a joyous month and season.

MONDAY — DECEMBER 2

WEATHER forecast: Snow — followed by little boys on sleds.

— *Henry Morgan*

Tuesday — December 3

Today Margaret and I have been busy setting out the house decorations for Advent. Years ago George made a wreath for our centrepiece on the dining room table. We found it again in Bruce's workshop, newly painted and cleaned for this new season.

We also set out the stable with a little straw and a few miniature animals. Each week we add a few more figures and on Christmas Day the youngest child visiting us places the baby Jesus in the crêche.

Wednesday — December 4

You are writing a gospel,
A chapter each day,
By deeds that you do,
By words that you say.
Men read what you write,
Whether faithless or true,
Say, what is the gospel according to you?

Thursday — December 5

A diplomat is one who can tell a man he's open minded when he means he has a hole in his head.

FRIDAY — DECEMBER 6

LIKE many people, today we mailed our out-of-town Christmas parcels. Last evening we spent many hours wrapping our gifts for family and friends who will not be with us during the holiday season.

I have been quite well organized this year. I have spent many spare minutes knitting, crocheting, or sewing small gifts for loved ones. I also picked up many more little things in the antique or craft stores in England.

This seems to keep the shopping in December from becoming too hectic. It also gives me more time to write letters to accompany each gift, a task that I greatly enjoy.

SATURDAY — DECEMBER 7

OLD age is the snow of the earth; it must, through light and truth, give warmth to the seeds of youth below, protecting them and fulfilling their purpose.

— *Kahlil Gibran*

SUNDAY — DECEMBER 8

AND she shall bring forth a son, and thou shalt call his name Jesus.

— *Matthew 1:21*

MONDAY — DECEMBER 9

I do not feel any age yet. There is no age to the spirit.

TUESDAY — DECEMBER 10

TODAY Bruce brought home a lovely red poinsettia, one of my favourite Christmas decorations. I always think of George when I see one.

WEDNESDAY — DECEMBER 11

I ask not more of pleasure or of joy
For this brief while —
But rather let me for the joys I have
Be glad and smile.

— *B.Y. Williams*

THURSDAY — DECEMBER 12

THE poinsettia plant is known as the Christmas flower. The legend says that a child knelt outside the stable in Bethlehem, afraid to enter because he had no gift. Suddenly a beautiful red plant rose at his feet. He picked it and offered it to the Holy Child. I enjoy the poinsettia even more because of the legend.

FRIDAY — DECEMBER 13

I am really quite excited today! Fred called me this morning to ask if I would like to join with his family this weekend in a trip to Black Creek Pioneer Village to celebrate an old fashioned Christmas.

Fred knows my weakness for he said, "I think you'll enjoy being with the boys on the sleigh ride singing carols, Gram."

How right he is! It brings back all the memories of sleigh rides with George in our first cutter, those many years ago. We would travel the route to church singing all the way. This will be a real trip down "memory lane" and I am so happy that they thought to include me.

SATURDAY — DECEMBER 14

THE only safe and sure way to destroy an enemy is to make him your friend.

SUNDAY — DECEMBER 15

THIS evening when I turned my radio on, I heard a portion of Handel's Messiah.

"For unto us a child is born, unto us a child is given . . . and his name shall be called Wonderful Counsellor, the mighty God, the everlasting Father, the Prince of Peace."

Monday — December 16

Once to every man and nation
Comes the moment to decide
In the strife of truth with falsehood,
For the good or evil side:
Some great cause, God's new Messiah,
Offering each the bloom or blight;
And the choice goes by for ever
'Twixt that darkness and that light.

— *James Russell Lowell*

Tuesday — December 17

From the time that mankind first observed birds, manned flight has been the subject of speculation and dreams.

In the art, literature, and mythology of so many cultures it soon becomes clear that the desire to fly was probably universal.

The Wright Brothers made their successful manned flight in their *Flyer* on December 17, 1903, and the dreams of hundreds of years became reality.

Wednesday — December 18

The real purpose of our existence is not to make a living, but to make a life — a worthy, well rounded, useful life.

Thursday — December 19

THERE is something so beautiful about the first real snowfall of the season. It always amazes me to wake and see that the whole world has turned white in just a few short hours. The branches are drooping low under their burden and our lawn looks like a new white quilt. I think I will walk before breakfast to take in the unspoiled beauty of it all.

Friday — December 20

I spent some time today packing Christmas hampers for some shut-in friends. How much pleasure I get from this task.

This afternoon we will have the fun of delivering our baskets to old friends. The Christmas joy really does come in giving, especially when you know how much your gifts are appreciated.

Saturday — December 21

'TIS winter, yet there is no sound along the air
Of winds along their battle-ground; but gently there
The snow is falling — all around.

— *Ralph Hoyt*

SUNDAY — DECEMBER 22

WE had a service of carols at church this morning. It was glorious to hear the sound of voices, young and old together, singing all of the old favourite Christmas hymns. One that I most enjoyed was "Once in Royal David's City."

Once in Royal David's city
Stood a lowly cattle shed,
Where a mother laid her baby
In a manger for His bed.
Mary was that mother mild,
Jesus Christ her little child.

MONDAY — DECEMBER 23

BRUCE brought home the Christmas tree this evening. It is a lovely scotch pine, a perfect symbol of the meaning of Christmas. The evergreen represents eternity, which Christ came to make real for us; the lights speak of Christ, light of the world; and the decorations declare the joy and happiness of Christ's birthday.

TUESDAY — DECEMBER 24

'TWAS the night before Christmas, when all through the house.
Not a creature was stirring — not even a mouse.

— *C.C. Moore*

WEDNESDAY — DECEMBER 25

CHRISTMAS Day is one of the most joyful celebrations in our Christian year. Every family has its own traditions and we are certainly no exception.

Our day begins very early with Marg putting the turkey in the oven to start cooking.

Bruce makes us a cup of tea and we open our gifts for each other. He then cooks up a big breakfast while Marg and I check that the table is completely set and that all the vegetables are ready to go on for dinner.

Church is next on our agenda and we join with our pastor and many friends and neighbours in celebrating the birth of our Saviour.

Following church, we have a quiet time at home as we await the arrival of the rest of the family at around one o'clock.

Once everyone has arrived our youngest child puts the Baby Jesus in the crêche and all of the children sing "Happy Birthday."

Bruce then chooses "elves" to distribute our gifts and this is a most exciting time for the children. They play with their cousins and new toys until Marg announces "Turkey's ready" at around four o'clock.

It is a hectic but joyful family time for us all. Merry Christmas to you and your family!

Thursday — December 26

THE closing hours approach of the old year.
His aged head is white, his face is sere.
Though cheerful yet, and will be to the last:
O may thy years as peacefully be passed
That age may find thee still with smiling eyes
That look with joy expectant to the skies.

Friday — December 27

I enjoyed this composition on grandparents written by one of Christie's pupils.

"A Grandmother is a lady who has no little children of her own so she likes other people's children. A Grandfather is a man grandmother. He goes for walks with boys and talks about fishing and tractors and like that. Grandparents don't have to do anything except be there. Also they are old so they should not play hard or run. It is enough if they drive us to the market where the pretend horse is and have lots of money ready. Or if they take us on a walk they slow down past the good things like pretty leaves and caterpillars.

When they read to us, they don't skip parts or mind if it is the same story all the time.

They make everybody feel good."

What a beautiful tribute.

Saturday — December 28

This morning Marg and I went shopping and made a visit to our favourite fruit market. As usual we bought fresh fruits and vegetables — citrus fruits, grapes, apples, lettuce, watercress, and fresh broccoli and cauliflower.

I know that I am a senior citizen and things have changed greatly but I find it hard to take all these foods for granted. All winter long fresh foods are available to us and I, for one, really enjoy fresh beans in December.

The cost of fresh foods is quite high but in cooking for only one I can usually afford a few of these fresh "treats" each week.

Sunday — December 29

This is a very old Canadian carol.

'Twas in the moon of winter time, when all the birds had fleld,
That mighty Gitchi Manitou sent angel choirs instead.
Before their light the stars grew dim and wandering hunters heard the hymn
Jesus your king is born Jesus is born in excelsis gloria.

— *Jean de Brebeuf*

Monday — December 30

Home is where affections bind
Gentle hearts in unison;
Where the voices all are kind,
Holding sweet communion!

Home is where the heart can rest
Safe from darkening sorrow;
Where the friends we love the best
Brighten every morrow!

Home is where the friends that love
To our hearts are given;
Where the blessings from above
Make it seem a heaven!

Home is where the stars will shine
In the skies above us!
Peeping brightly through the vine,
Trained by those who love us.

Yes 'tis home, where smiles of cheer
Wreathe the brows that greet us;
And the one of all most dear
Ever comes to meet us!

TUESDAY — DECEMBER 31

NEW Year's Eve is a time for remembrance and a time for anticipation. Don't let it pass lightly.

We need to recall our many blessings and achievements of 1985 with gratitude; we need to acknowledge our disappointments and the grace that enabled us to handle them.

As 1986 draws near we anticipate the new year with faith and hope and thankfulness and we pray that with God's help we can make this coming year one of our happiest.

Happy New Year to all of you my friends!